The Time Minder

Ruth Wagner Miller

CHRISTIAN HERALD BOOKS
Chappaqua, New York

Verses marked TLB are taken from The Living Bible, copyright 1971 by Tyndale House Publishers, Wheaton, Ill. Used by permission.

Library of Congress Cataloging in Publication Data

Miller, Ruth W
　　The time minder.

　　　1. Home economics.　　2. Time allocation—Moral and religious aspects.　　3. Women—Religious life.
I.　Title.
TX147.M63　　　248'.4　　　79-55677
ISBN 0-915684-53-5

To Chuck,
who makes the time worthwhile

Contents

INTRODUCTION

I have not always used my time well. Nor have I ever been speedy. In fact, I was so slow climbing aboard the school bus as a child that the driver dubbed me "Grandma"—a name which my family still uses to tease me when I ponder something too long.

My first memory of the beauty of orderliness comes from a college philosophy course—"Introduction to Logic"—where I learned that: A—If oranges are round, and B—blocks are square, then C—oranges are not blocks. Logical thinking, helped along by an engineer-type husband even more deliberate than I, became a way of life (most of the time).

The necessity for planning came to the fore as I denmothered nine Cub scouts in perpetual motion. Those Den Mothers who failed to plan either had nervous breakdowns or their Cubs fell by the wayside, frustrated.

Establishing priorities and setting goals became part of my life when God called me to minister to the internationals in our community. Just a vague "I want to put God first" was no longer enough. In order to launch a conversational English school in our church, I was going to have to hoe around one cotton plant instead of trying to hoe the whole patch. I had to learn to say no without offending people. I learned to trust God when the interruptions came—and come they did, as internationals needing help called at all hours.

Many women have asked me to write this book. My one fear is that readers will dismiss it by saying, "Well, she's just one of those high energy people," or "I'm just not that well-organized."

To the first statement I protest, "I'm not! I'm not!" My round little Pennsylvania Dutch endomorphic body cries out, "Sit down! Read a book. Work on your needlepoint," as it fights me every step. Because of diabetes, I can't grab a candy bar for a quick energy pick-up, and I must pace myself so that my strength and my food intake match up. Between rising early and retiring late I have to squeeze in an afternoon nap.

To the second statement I say, "You can be. You can be." We women have been sold the idea that organization and efficiency make us unfeminine. I, too, like to look, smell, and act like a lady. But the idea that God's woman should be an empty-headed ornament is simply not scriptural.

As I have taught courses and led retreats for women, they have said, over and over again, "We want to have more time for the incorruptible treasures. Teach us how." And that's what this book is all about.

1 Viewing with Alarm

We women disagree about a lot of things these days—job versus home, children versus career, volunteer work versus a salary. But we do agree about one thing. Time. There's never enough of it.

We never quite fit the tasks crying for attention into the time allotted for getting them done. One job spills over into the next one's time slot until we've rolled a snowball we can scarcely push. No matter how we hurry, something remains unfinished.

Because we spend so much time on what needs doing, we seldom have time to do things we want to do. We see our dreams of creating a work of art, learning a new skill, improving our minds, or even snatching an hour for a game of tennis receding behind a pile of dirty laundry—and we resent it. On hot summer days we have to wear a top with sleeves because we haven't had time to shave our underarms. We find ourselves wishing gloves were back in fashion so we could hide our need for a manicure. We rebel at never having a moment to ourselves.

Then, one day, we notice how a friend has aged. We

11

peer in the mirror for telltale signs—wrinkles, gray hair—and sure enough, we see them. Our muscles ache after a gardening session. Someone our age dies and we're frightened. Our biblical three-score and ten years shrinks to two score or less. We panic and promise ourselves to make better use of what time is left to us. Then the telephone rings and we're off and running again. We can never seem to take the time to make time.

Frustrated? No doubt. Even desperate at times. But what can a woman with a family or a job or both; or an aging parent; or all of the above, do? Surely she's not to blame for her lack of control of her time. Or is she?

Most of us can't stand for someone else to control our kitchens. We fight excessive government control of our health and welfare. We bridle when someone tells us how to raise our children. Why is it, then, that we allow others to dictate the use of our time? Could it be that we don't understand what time is?

ATTITUDES, RIGHT AND WRONG

The biggest fallacy in our thinking about time has to do with the amount we get. The statement, "She has more time than I do," reflects this misconception. Each of us gets 24 hours a day—no more, no less. Each hour is equally divided into 60 minutes, 3600 seconds. The difference comes in how we allot our 24 hours. "She" may get more use out of her 3600 seconds per hour, but she gets not one second more.

How we regard our time will probably determine how we spend it. The Bible tells us that:

1. God created time. "Then God said, 'Let there be light.' And light appeared. And God was pleased with

it, and divided the light from the darkness. So he let it shine for awhile, and then there was darkness again. He called the light 'daytime,' and the darkness 'night-time.' Together they formed the first day....Then God said, 'Let there be bright lights in the sky to give light to the earth and to identify the day and the night; they shall bring about the seasons on the earth, and mark the days and years.' And so it was" (Gen. 1:3–5, 14–15, TLB).

2. Time belongs to God. "Day and night alike belong to you; you made the starlight and the sun" (Psalm 74:16, TLB).

3. God will give us all the time we need. "My God shall supply all your need according to his riches in glory by Christ Jesus" (Phil. 4:19, KJV).

4. God expects us to use our time wisely. "So be careful how you act; these are difficult days. Don't be fools; be wise: make the most of every opportunity you have for doing good" (Eph. 5:15–16, TLB). "Make the best possible use of your time" (Col. 4:5, Phillips).

5. We will be asked to account for how we have spent our time. "For the man who uses well what he is given shall be given more, and he shall have abundance. But from the man who is unfaithful, even what little responsibility he has shall be taken from him" (Matt. 25:29, TLB).

Our time belongs to God just as our money, our talents, and our children do. He allows us to use it for a little while. When we acknowledge His ownership of our time, we recognize that He also has the responsibility for stretching it to fit our needs. His promise to supply "all our need" (Phil. 4:19)—including all the time we need—relieves us from worry about not having enough. We need to learn to differentiate between time needed and time desired. When we let God in on our need, He gives us the time to cover it. He doesn't necessarily give us a greater number of minutes, but He does help us use the minutes we have more efficiently, and He multiplies the quality of what we produce in the time we do have.

Because God expects wise use of our time and will ask us to account for it, I want to make sure that I'm the one who decides how I spend mine. Too many others have too many ideas of how I should spend my time. If I have not thought it through, have not planned its use, then by my own default, someone else will decide for me.

This is not to say that I don't have obligations that take up my time—I do. But those obligations are of my choosing, not someone else's. For example, housework. I can either regard it through martyr's eyes as an unpleasant chore foisted on me by society, or I can admit that I entered marriage with my eyes wide open, knowing what would be expected of me. In our era of change and redefined roles, I can opt out of housework any time I want. I can get a job, hire a maid, or put the children in a day nursery. I can even go so far as to divorce my husband or desert my family. When I choose housework over any of these alternatives, I elect to spend a certain portion of my time at it.

Because I control my time and answer to God for its wise use, I take responsibility for the choices I make. I must continually sort the opportunities available to me and sift out those which do not fit into the life-plan God has shown me.

When faced with an overwhelming number of obligations and a limited amount of time, I must ask myself: Is time the problem or am I the problem? I must manage my time, but I will never do this until I learn to manage myself.

2 Where Do I Want to Wind Up?

ESTABLISHING PRIORITIES

Those in management circles would call the sorting and sifting mentioned in the last chapter "establishing priorities." My priorities become the basis on which I make choices—not only of how to spend time, but also where to spend my money, and even how to conduct myself.

Just as in controlling my time (if I don't decide how to spend my time, someone else will do it for me), others are only too happy to impose their priorities on me. When they do, I lose control of my life; but God never relieves me of the responsibility. I can never use someone else's priorities as an excuse for my action or inaction. I may willingly make someone else's top priority one of mine, but it must be my choice.

How do you determine priorities? Ask yourself what is really important to you. Write it down. Talk to God about it. Ask His advice, then trust Him to show you.

For example, my own priorities are: my relationship with God (and in a way, this determines the others); care of the family God has given me; the building up of the faith of other Christians; helping other women to realize their potential in Jesus Christ; and loving people into the Kingdom of God. I have arrived at these over a period of time. They are the yardstick by which I measure whether or not something is worth spending my time on. When having to make a choice on how to spend a day, an hour, a minute, these are my guidelines:

1. Have I spent time with God today?
2. Have I taken care of my family's needs?
3. Will it help build up someone's faith?
4. Will it introduce someone to Jesus Christ?

I offer my own priorities only as an example. I do not presume to dictate what yours may be. I do recommend that you write yours down—first, so you don't forget them, and second, as an act of commitment between you and God. Tell Him these are your priorities and that with His help you will make your choices based upon them.

We sometimes hear the expression, "She'd better get her priorities in order." Often what the speaker means is that "she" had the audacity to say no to one of the speaker's pet projects. "She" may already have established her priorities, and that's what caused her to say no. We must be careful not to hang our priorities on someone else.

Once I line up my priorities and try to live by them, I run the risk of being criticized and misunderstood by others. But I must set my own priorities and try not to let someone else's groundless displeasure with them influence me.

SETTING GOALS

Someone once said you have to know what you want to accomplish in a day before you can decide what time to set the alarm clock for. This deciding is goal setting.

When I think of goals and priorities, I think of the third little pig in the children's fable *The Three Little Pigs*. He had self-preservation as his highest priority. To that end he built a house that the wolf couldn't blow down. Being a pig, he probably had goals of living comfortably and having plenty to eat. He needed to go to the fair, buy food, and get back home before the time at which he had agreed to meet the wolf. To accomplish this, he set his alarm clock to waken him an hour earlier. This pig had set his priorities. His goals determined his time schedule.

Usable goals must be both measurable and attainable. They must state what you want to accomplish in terms that can be evaluated. For example, that little pig went to the fair to buy his food. If he had stated his goal as "providing one of the basic necessities of life," how would he know when he'd reached it? But if his goal was to have enough food in the house to outlast the wolf, he moved closer to something he could act on. When he set as his goal "to buy a bushel of corn," he moved into the realm of measurable and attainable.

The man who says, "My life goal is to get rich," may never know when he gets there. But the one who says, "My life goal is to make a million dollars," can chart his progress.

For a goal to be attainable, it must be realistic. Why set yourself a goal of becoming a jockey if you're well over six feet tall?

Take the time now to set some life goals for yourself. Ask God what goals He wants you to have. Start by completing this sentence: "By the end of my life I want to _____ ."

Reaching Goals

Once you have set life goals, move purposefully toward them. How? How do you eat an elephant? One bite at a time. You do the same with your life goals. Examine your elephant, and cut off a leg or an ear to work on. This will be your goal for one year. Write it down, always asking for and expecting God's guidance in your decision.

Eating a leg or an ear of an elephant is still a pretty big chore. You're apt to choke or give up. This is when you need to take up knife and fork and cut yourself a bite that you can chew on for a whole month—your monthly goal. Write it down. Then analyze it. When should you begin? How much time should you allow? When you finally get that bite to the point where you can swallow it, you know that elephant will never be the same size again. You've made a start.

You can use this method of goal setting in every area of your life—spiritual, physical, mental, family. For example, in the spiritual realm one of my goals is to know God better and better. To do this, I must learn to pray. I set that as a one year goal. Since I must know what God says about prayer, I set a one-month goal of looking up, with the aid of a concordance, every Scripture reference on prayer. This goal is measurable and attainable. I'll know when I've finished it. Then I'll take the next bite, which might be experimenting with the forms of prayer or keeping a prayer notebook.

What has goal setting to do with time? I no longer feel that time controls me. I know where I'm going. I've decided what I must do to get there, and be it ever so small a segment of the task, I've chosen to spend my time on it.

Priorities and goals must be flexible. As our circumstances or our values change, some things will grow less important; others will take on more meaning. By discussing our goals and priorities with God periodically, we keep them current and applicable to today's situations.

3 Calendars Come Before Clocks

The oft-quoted management axiom, "If you fail to plan, you plan to fail," aptly describes the difference between the successful person and the marginal operator. The tycoons of business and industry leave as little to chance as possible. They establish goals and make concrete plans for reaching them. They think through the "what ifs" and allow for contingencies. They do not let fear of the future paralyze them. They make alternate plans.

Why don't Christians—from the overworked pastor, just starting his sermon late Saturday night, to the harried housewife, pressing a shirt at 8:00 A.M. while her husband stands by in his underwear, waiting to snatch it off the ironing board—plan better? Or plan at all? It's a poor general who marches his troops into battle without considering what his enemy will do and how he can safely withdraw his forces if it becomes necessary.

Yet we who engage in holy warfare often march into the daily fray with few or no battle plans. Do we feel that we can live in a haphazard manner, and it will all

20

come right in the end? This attitude contradicts the concept of discipleship.

The word *disciple* has the same root as the word *discipline*—ordered, regulated. God's true disciple disciplines (regulates) her life—her appetites, her attitudes, her actions. She regulates the use of her time by planning.

God expects us to plan. "We should make our plans—counting on God to direct us" (Prov. 16:9, TLB). "But don't begin until you count the cost. For who would begin construction of a building without first getting estimates and then checking to see if he has enough money to pay the bills?" (Luke 14:28, TLB).

To plan our work effectively, we need to think through each task, applying the following management planning procedures:

1. Define the task.
2. Set deadline.
3. Establish procedures.
4. Procure materials.
5. Estimate length of time to complete task, and set start-up time.
6. Activate plan.
7. Evaluate results.

A simple illustration of this might be baking a birthday cake where I:

1. Define the task—bake a birthday cake.
2. Set deadline—May 30, 2:00 P.M.
3. Establish procedures—measure, mix, bake, cool cake; measure, mix frosting; decorate cake.
4. Procure materials—cake and frosting ingredients, right size pans, cooling racks, electric mixer, cake plate, candles.
5. Set starting time—total time required for assem-

bling, mixing, baking, cooling, mixing frosting, and decorating, plus time for interruptions, equals four hours. Begin no later than 10:00 A.M., preferably sooner.

This planning eliminates running next door to borrow the right size pan or driving to the market to buy eggs. It avoids having the decorations slide off the cake because it was too warm when frosted.

But beware! A little planning leads to more. I must ask the child which flavor cake he wants and think out how to decorate it. I must plan the shopping trip to buy ingredients prior to 10:00 A.M. I plan what to do around the house during the thirty minutes the cake bakes and during the cooling time.

TYPES OF PLANS

This sort of continuous looking ahead illustrates three types of planning we need to do—long-range (remember cake, gifts, card); intermediate-range (buy ingredients and candles while shopping); and short-range (bake birthday cake today, wrap gifts while cake is in the oven).

Here's how I use these stages of planning:

Long-range planning involves being aware of future events, making a note of dates, and setting in motion any long-term activities. Using a planning calendar, I fill in:

1. Special occasions—birthdays, anniversaries, camps, vacations, speaking engagements, editorial deadlines, and any other dates I know about.

2. Regular commitments—meetings, choir rehearsals, gardening schedules. These all require time that I can't spend on other projects.

3. Segments of my goals which I would like to see accomplished by certain times. I start translating my goals into accomplishments when I plan steps to achieve them.

This, my master plan, tells me what *intermediate-range* plans I must make. As far-off dates draw closer I begin to think about specific tasks. I plot out the six planning steps for each event. I write the actions for specific days on my planning calendar.

Some people restrict their long-range planning to a year and their intermediate planning to a month. Whatever works best is fine. My long-range plan extends as far out into the future as I know firm dates. My intermediate plans revolve around the seasons. Summer is garden and vacation time. Fall begins school, football, band, the new church year. Winter includes the holidays, special music, houseguests. Spring brings on a flurry of year-end school activities and garden planting.

My *short-range* plans cover the current month. I keep a notebook with one page for each day of the month. I fill in every detail I can think of that will require an outlay of my time—including housework and time for personal care (haircuts, etc.). I do this at the beginning of the month and add to the plans as the month progresses. My calendar page for today includes: phone calls; checks to mail; dry cleaner pickup; a writers' meeting; a trip to the garden store, the fabric shop, and the sock outlet (they're on the same side of town as my meeting); regular hours to write (moving toward my goal of completing this book by a certain date); and a note that our son will play in the orchestra tonight (this determines the time I must serve dinner).

Each calendar page serves as the basis for making

my daily schedule. When the day is over, I glance over the next day's activities, decide what clothes I'll wear, and check them for condition. I learned (the hard way) to do this one day when I had planned to wear an outfit requiring boots, only to find, the morning of the meeting, that the boots needed polishing. I arrived for my meeting late and with polish-stained fingernails. Having a plan and sticking to it avoids overcrowding everybody's schedule or forgetting important events.

Our priorities help us choose what we want to do. Our goals give us a sense of direction. And our planning makes us move in that direction in an orderly fashion.

◿ Beat the Clock

I know of no greater need for God's direction than in the scheduling of my daily life. "We should make plans—counting on God to direct us" (Prov. 16:9, TLB). "Commit your work to the Lord, then it will succeed" (Prov. 16:3, TLB). Ahead of the actual writing down of my time commitments comes a prayer of commitment giving the day back to God, acknowledging my stewardship of it, and asking His direction in its use.

When making out my daily schedule, I want to account for every minute. I have lost years—one minute at a time. The hours really do take care of themselves when we take care of the minutes. By utilizing fragments of time, we can often complete a big job piecemeal. Too often we refuse to tackle a job because it will take more time than we have. By breaking the job down into smaller components, we can whittle away at it.

One of my friends has the slogan, "Something is better than nothing." Applying that to the use of our time, we can get satisfaction from finishing small segments of a job instead of bemoaning our lack of time to do the whole thing. I doubt if I will ever again have enough time to clean my kitchen from baseboard to ceiling. Yet by cleaning one drawer, one cupboard, one refrigerator shelf every time I make a phone call, I manage to completely clean the whole kitchen far more often than the traditional spring and fall cleaning that upset the household and left me exhausted.

Scheduling the day means writing it down. This does three things. It helps us to see the blocks of time, gives us a sense of accomplishment when we cross off a completed task, and provides us with a record of how we've spent the day. Should someone ask, "What did you do today?" we can show him the day's plan instead of answering, "I don't know what I did, but it took me all day."

I like to use a book called *Day at a Glance* for my daily scheduling. It has a page for each day, with a line for every fifteen minute segment of the day. That way I have a permanent record of when I did what. When did I get my hair cut? Feed the orchids? Clean the carpet? It's all there. In the days before *Day at a Glance*, I just used the back of an envelope.

My short-range plan page (from my notebook) tells me what I must get done that day. I fill in these time blocks on the schedule first, including any transportation time. Mornings are my brain time (writing, studying, researching, answering mail); afternoons are brawn time (housework, gardening, errands); and evening is family time (when they don't need me I sew or read). Next, I block in mealtimes—preparation, serving, and cleanup. Because my notebook page for the day lists small segments from each of my monthly goals, I automatically spend some time each day working toward each goal.

BE REALISTIC

When planning the daily schedule, be realistic about the amount of time required to do a job. Not allowing enough time causes one task to run over into the time allotted for the next. This snowballs until we get frustrated or frantic. As the Pennsylvania Dutch housewife put it, "The hurrier I go, the behinder I get." Your realism should include some leeway for interruptions.

If the time available doesn't cover the time needed to do a job, anticipate that and plan to accomplish only a portion of the task. This lets you remain in control of your time. With your priorities established and your goals segmented into attainable portions, you'll know that your planning includes the important things of life.

Having planned your work, now work your plan. But expect interruptions. They will come whether you plan for them or not.

We can look on interruptions as annoying, frustrating blockades to our best-laid plans, or we can think of them as God's little nudgings. "We can make our plans, but the final outcome is in God's hands" (Prov. 16:1, TLB). "When all kinds of trials and temptations crowd into your lives, my brothers, don't resent them as intruders, but welcome them as friends" (James 1:2, Phillips). Having committed your schedule to God at the beginning of the day, look carefully at each interruption, asking God, "What is it You want me to learn from this, Father?"

Charlie Shedd, in his book *Time for All Things*, has a chapter entitled, "I Will Make Friends With Divine Interruptions," in which he says, "One of the marks of true Christian greatness will be a certain 'interruptibility.' This life has an elastic quality. It is equipped with expansion points. Already containing many interests, such a soul has room for one more real need if it comes from higher up."

As I write this, the high school band director has just phoned to ask if I can get someone to drive sixty miles this afternoon to pick up two bass drums. This means at least a thirty-minute interruption to make phone calls, not to mention the broken train of thought. Yet, my husband and I accepted the copresidency of the band booster club as our mission to the immediate community. It fits into my priorities of serving my family (we have a child in the band and one coming up) and of loving people into the Kingdom of God. (Where is there a greater need for God's love made visible than in a large high school? And how can we permeate the school with His love if we're not available?) The opportunities for providing a positive witness don't always come according to my schedule. But God's schedule? You bet.

Not all interruptions come from God. Some arrive special delivery straight from hell. But we can turn these, too, into victories by offering them up to God and asking Him to use them. Our refusal to grow irritable over interruptions is itself a victory.

BEAT THE CLOCK

If we think about and analyze our work habits, we can learn to do most tasks in less time, thereby winning for ourselves a few extra minutes from each job. Too often, especially with routine things, we daydream as we do them instead of concentrating on the job at hand.

I like to play a little game called "Beat the Clock." I look at the time allotted to do a job (running the sweeper, for instance); then I set the kitchen timer for five minutes less than that time. I fly into action, thinking and concentrating on that job, and find I can often chop off a few minutes.

C. N. Parkinson, in his book *Parkinson's Law*, states that "Work expands so as to fill the time available for its completion . . . the thing to be done swells in importance and complexity in a direct ratio with the time to be spent." A little old lady may take an hour to write a post card—selecting just the right card, stamp, color of ink, and words—because she has nothing better to do. A busy executive will write a post card in three minutes because that's all the time he has available. Playing "Beat the Clock" helps me reverse Parkinson's Law to "Work can be compressed into the time available for its completion."

We must forever analyze, evaluate, and streamline our systems. Periodically, take stock of that mountain of chores and ask yourself:

1. Is there a faster way to do this? (After thirteen years, I have just rearranged some kitchen cupboards because I saw a system which would allow me to unload the dishwasher more efficiently.)

2. Does this task need doing at all? Am I doing this just because I've always done it or because my mother always did it? The classic example of this is the housewife who always cut an inch off each end of her roast before cooking it. When her husband asked her why she did it, she replied, "Well, my mother always did." When the mother was asked why she cut an inch off each end of the roast, the mother said, "Honey, I don't know why you do it, but my roasting pan is two inches too short."

3. Could someone else do it as well or better? (Your children, maybe?)

4. Can it be postponed? (Make sure you postpone for priority's sake and not just for procrastination.)

Time and motion study experts stand with stopwatch in hand and look for more efficient traffic patterns. We need to do the same. But we can call on God to show His ways for best using His time.

EVALUATE

At the end of the day, look over your schedule. What didn't you get done? Why? Did you have control over the situation? How did God work through the interruptions? Do you need to reschedule something for the next day, or didn't it need doing after all?

Then, instead of staying awake, worrying over what we didn't get done today and what faces us tomorrow, we can drift off into well-earned sleep. For we know that today we reduced several elephants by a mouthful and tomorrow, through careful planning and scheduling and God's guidance, we will take another bite.

5 Streamlining Repetitive Chores

Some of the chores we women have to do keep repeating themselves with maddening regularity. For instance, I haven't yet found a way to clean the shower once and for all. Oh, I could declare it off limits. But then I've smelled our son after a soccer game, and I'm not sure I want to go that far. My choice of being a housewife includes doing repetitive chores (and I can't abolish them altogether), so the next best thing is to get them over with as quickly as possible and move on to more pleasant activities. To do this I need a schedule and a system.

For the remainder of this book, you'll be reading those two words, schedule and system, often, because I apply them to everything from housework to cooking to applying my war paint to talking with God.

HAVE A SCHEDULE

Some household jobs like washing curtains don't need doing very often. We tend to forget them until company's coming, when we begin to look at things with a more critical eye. Then it's too late. Other chores are so distasteful that we ignore them as long as possible. I tend to put off washing windows until they're so bad every day looks rainy. To avoid these extremes and the haunting feeling that you'll never get it all done, put your cleaning projects on a schedule.

Having the schedule assures me that I will eventually get everything done. It keeps me from stopping in the middle of one job to start another that I've noticed needs doing. I know that the job is on the schedule and will come up for attention at the proper time. Right now, we have a bulging catch-all closet that is threatening to tear the door off its hinges and send an avalanche out into the hall. Because that closet is on this Friday's schedule, I can stop feeling guilty about it and get on with more important things.

My schedule also acts as a whip at times, forcing me to take action when the old me would rather let it go.

To make a schedule for your home, walk through the house, clipboard in hand, and list all the cleaning jobs that you see. Now sit down and decide how often you should do them. Try to be realistic. Few American women scrub their doorsteps every day. And few American husbands expect them to. What is important to you? A little dust doesn't bother me when just the family is here, but clutter drives me bonkers. What it amounts to is that I'd rather pick up than dust.

Next, make out a schedule of yearly, twice-yearly, quarterly, monthly, weekly, and daily chores. To do this, you must also decide when it makes the most sense to do a job. That is, when in a time sense and when in relationship to other tasks. My cleaning schedule looks like this:

> Yearly   Clean carpeting. We do this in September, after the children are back in school but it's still warm enough to have the air condition-

er running or the windows open to speed up drying

Twice-yearly 1. Wash curtains
2. Vacuum walls. Do in October (after the spiders have come in for the winter) and April (after furnace gets turned off). Best done while curtains are down for washing
3. Wash window screens—May and November
4. Wash light fixtures—June and December
5. Rub furniture with oil—January and July
6. Refurbish house plants—March and September

Quarterly Wash windows—January, April, July, October

Monthly 1. Vacuum woodwork—first week
2. Vacuum drapes and upholstery—second week
3. Vacuum closet floors—third week
4. Clean a drawer or a closet shelf—fourth and fifth weeks

Weekly 1. Vacuum and dust
2. Scrub bathrooms
3. Mop kitchen floor
4. Clean oven
5. Clean refrigerator
6. Sweep garage and front step

Daily 1. Pick up
2. Make beds
3. Do laundry

    4. Sweep kitchen, vacuum high traffic areas
as needed

    5. Wash dishes

I've further subdivided these duties so that I do a little of each one every day instead of doing it all on one day. I cope with monthly and weekly duties like this:

Monday—Clean master bedroom and bath. This means change linens, vacuum, and dust. The first Monday of the month I include the monthly "first week" chore of vacuuming the woodwork. The second Monday I vacuum drapes and upholstery. I even subdivide scrubbing the shower walls by scrubbing one wall each week. None of these monthly tasks takes more than ten minutes, but if I were to do it all in one day, they'd have to call an ambulance for me.

Tuesday—Clean children's rooms and bath using same system.

Wednesday—Clean living room, dining room, hall, and stairway.

Thursday—Clean kitchen, enclosed porch, and downstairs playroom.

Friday—Surface clean for the weekend and clean garage.

After a while the schedule becomes second nature, and I just need to remind myself which week it is. I do those twice-yearly and quarterly jobs during the third and fourth weeks of the month, attending to each room on its assigned day. I wash the master bedroom curtains and vacuum the walls on the Monday of the week scheduled for curtains and walls, the children's curtains and walls on Tuesday of that week, and so forth.

It helps to put those semi-annual and quarterly jobs on the planning calendar. Then, when someone calls and wants me to do something that day, I know to say, "I'm sorry, but I already have something scheduled."

I hate having the house all torn up. My family hates it even more. By taking very small bites of this elephant I manage to keep it under control. But the best part is, I seldom spend more than an hour a day cleaning house, and I can stand almost anything for an hour. Then I'm free to spend the rest of my time in more appealing ways.

HAVE A SYSTEM

Devising a system takes time, but it is time well-spent. First, analyze what needs to be done. Then plan how to do it. In his book *Executive Housekeeping*, Auren Uris suggests that you describe each job using action verbs (go, lift, wash, scrub), then apply the following "why" questions to each verb:

1. Why is it necessary?
2. Why in that place?
3. Why at that time?
4. Why by this person (instead of a helper)?
5. Why in this manner?

When you can't give a satisfactory answer to a "why" question, chances are you can improve on the procedure.

When I applied his method of analysis to cleaning the bathroom, it went like this:

Ruth: Go downstairs to get cleaning supplies.
Uris question #1: Why is it necessary?
Ruth: Because that's where I store them.
Uris question #2: Why in that place?
Ruth: Because I've always kept them there.

And right there I stopped. For thirteen years I'd been going to the basement to fetch my supplies. On my next trip to the store I invested in a bowl brush, a can of cleanser, and a sponge for each bathroom. By keeping the supplies where I use them, I save myself two trips up and down the stairs. By keeping the supplies at hand I also make it possible for each person using the bath to clean up after himself.

As a part of your cleaning system, move through the house or a room in the same order every time. By doing this you can develop a mental and physical rhythm to your movements which enables you to perform pick up and cleaning chores automatically. This frees your mind for other things and lets you use your time twice. While vacuuming you can think up a kindness to perform for someone or plan out what to write in a letter. If you'll keep a note pad and pencil in your apron (or in my case, blue jeans) pocket, you can jot down thoughts as they come to you. Then, when you sit down for lunch, transfer your notes to the appropriate planning pages of your notebook.

To establish this rhythm to your cleaning, treat each room as a circle. Move around the circle clockwise or counterclockwise, always starting in the same place. Right-handed people usually move counterclockwise, picking up and doing more with the right hand. The natural movement of hand and arm is circular, toward the center of the body. Lefties reverse the process.

Pick up, straighten, put away as you go. Try not to crisscross the room. If you pick up something that belongs on the other side of the room, hang onto it until you get around to that spot. If you have a lot of clutter, you may need to carry a basket to hold things. Get a basket with a handle so that you can carry it over your arm and free both hands. Use your basket to collect items which belong in other rooms, too.

After picking up in one room, proceed to the adjacent room, using the circle idea to move quickly from room to room throughout the house. Upon entering each room, check your basket to see if it contains items you want to deliver there. Stay ahead of the clutter by making this grand tour every day.

When cleaning a room, use the circle system for vacuuming, dusting, and mopping. This way you avoid going over a spot the second time. Bring the circle idea right on down to scrubbing the tub, or oven, or even a burnt-on pan. The idea is to establish a system, a regular route.

One last word about your system. Don't get so locked into it that you're paralyzed if somebody's in the spot where you want to start. You want your system to be a tool, not a tyrant.

Speaking of tools—now is the time to have a look at yours. Do you have the right tool for the job? Does its size fit the job, and does its size fit your size? Scrubbing with too small a brush makes for a slow cleanup, but a brush which is too large for your hand causes muscle fatigue and may make you quit before the job is completed.

Plan to replace worn-out equipment as fast as you can afford to. I find that a new broom not only sweeps cleaner, but it also boosts my morale.

While you're at it, take stock of your cleaning supplies. Do you still use the same types of waxes and polishes that you started housekeeping with? Why? Get in the habit of checking out new products when you see them advertised. Not every cleaner will be better just because it's new, but the law of averages is on your side, and sooner or later you'll find a winner. When you do, it will save precious time and energy.

By the same token, get rid of all the cleaning supplies and gadgets you've acquired that don't really do the job for you. Keep only those that you currently use. When you open the last bottle or package of a cleaning product, make a note on your shopping list to buy another. Nothing slows you down more than getting out all the brushes, pails, and rags, only to find that the cleanser can is empty.

HAVE HELP

When we ask ourselves the planning question "Can this job be done as well or better by someone else?" about housework, we have to answer "yes." Granted, we may have to give up some of our ideas about perfection. We will certainly have to get used to someone else's way of doing things. But help is available—hired or otherwise.

Some women feel that hiring a maid is an admission of their inability to cope with the job. Others don't want the bother of training someone. Still others can't find a maid who meets their standards of perfection. But here we're talking about ways to have more time, and for that you can't beat having someone else do the job.

If you can afford it, hire help. If you can't afford it, sit down and figure out what you can give up in order to have enough money to pay for help. A maid may save you time that you can then use to economize elsewhere. We have help one day a week. She does the surface cleaning to get us ready for the weekend, freeing my Fridays for other things. She saves me enough time so that I make most of the clothes for our family. Doing this, I save enough money to pay for the maid. It's a trade-off. All things being equal, I'd rather sew and garden than vacuum.

Some women think that if only they had a maid, all their problems would go away. Not so. I know women with full-time live-in domestic help who still can't get it together. Failing to organize their own lives, they haven't organized their help, either. Most household helpers have not studied the principles of time management and work efficiency. They do what they're told to do, and when not directed, they do the best they can.

If you have or would like to have hired help, here are my suggestions for keeping her happy and yourself at peace with the situation.

1. Pay her fairly and treat her well. The Bible tells us, as employers, to treat those who work for us with the same respect and fairness that we want from them (Eph. 6:9).

2. You work out the schedule and system for cleaning your house. Then write it down for her. Don't expect her to read your mind.

3. See that she has good tools and cleaning supplies and knows how to use them efficiently. Show her.

4. Ask her for suggestions. If she works for other people, she may have picked up some good ideas or learned about some better products. But don't feel that you must always take her suggestions. Remember that you are the employer, and keep your relationship on a businesslike basis for both your sakes.

5. Don't expect her to do more in a day than you could do. In fact, she will probably do less.

6. Having shown her how you want a job done, accept that she may prefer to do it her own way. Live

with it if you can. Our maid works like crazy in the morning so that she can fold laundry while watching her favorite soap opera in the afternoon.

7. The presence of a maid will not relieve you of having to clean up in between. Unless your household consists of one very neat adult, the carpet will still get littered, the dishes will still get dirty, and the bathtub will still scum up. At best, she can only do part of what needs doing. It's a well-known axiom that if you've left it all for the maid to do on her day, the day you're planning a party she'll have car trouble and not show up.

If you have enough children and they have enough time, you can organize them into an efficient work force. This has the added advantage of training them in skills you should be teaching them anyway. Of course, it's easier and quicker to do a job yourself than to train someone else to do it. But we're talking about the long haul, and good management principles have always dictated the training of others and the delegating of responsibilities.

When your children are working for you, they can't be out earning money by babysitting or mowing lawns. Yet they, too, need money. They should be compensated for their work beyond their regular chores and treated as well as any other employee.

To cut down on the insistent ticking of those repetitive chores, schedule, systematize, and (whenever possible) delegate.

6 Keeping Their Shirts On

Although God looks on the heart, man looks on the outward appearance. How well I dress myself and my family has direct bearing on what people think of us. And I care what people think. My husband's success in his business, our children's acceptance by their teachers and cohorts, and my sense of well-being and self-respect—all are directly influenced by our appearance. People observe our clothes and how we wear them long before they get close enough to us to see the warmth of our smiles.

Granted, then, that we want to look as good as we can. But the clothes closet can trap us into wasting time and money. It can drive us into panic when, because of the lack of a system and a schedule, we can't wear what we wanted to wear because it's dirty or torn. Bulging clothes closets do us no good if everything there looks like a candidate for the rag bag.

Anticipate your family's clothing needs and work them into your plans. Remember those long, intermediate, and short-range plans? They should include your plans to clothe your family. Will your daughter need a new outfit this fall? Long-range plans should show it. Intermediate-range plans need to allow time for choosing patterns and fabric. Short-range plans provide time to make it or buy it—well ahead of the day she needs it. Planning helps eliminate those emergency shopping trips when you're apt, in your desperation, to buy the inappropriate. Unnecessary trips for impulsive purchases waste time, energy, and money.

Once you've acquired the clothes in styles and colors that look best on you (more about that in a later chapter), you want to keep them in a constant state of ready-to-wear. That means clean and mended. And that means laundry.

HAVE A SYSTEM

Are you the type who does the laundry when the hamper gets so full that the lid won't stay down? Or the type who has to stand there holding a hair dryer on your son's band uniform because you didn't wash it soon enough? I write from experience, remember. Or perhaps you still do the old "Monday is wash day" bit—a carryover from when wives had to fire up the wash kettle in the backyard. Of course they had to do it all in one day. They made their own soap, too. That doesn't mean we have to.

Doing all the laundry on one day is a fine system if it is your system and not something you inherited from your mother. The system works only if your family members have enough clothes to last a week. Ours don't, and won't until they stop growing.

My laundry system involves washing fewer clothes but doing it more often. Each morning, I take a load of clothes to the laundry area. While the washing machine fills, I inspect and pretreat stains. I also fold any clothes that I've dried on the drying rack the day before. I add the detergent, then load in the clothes. Total elapsed time—less than five minutes. The laundry needs no further attention until I'm ready to dry it.

In good weather, I sometimes get very virtuous and hang the laundry outside to save electricity, but this takes time. To do it, I must make an allowance in the schedule. In order to line-dry the clothes, I have to hang them out early in the day. Usually, I'm long gone or into another project when the washing machine stops, and I don't like being controlled by my washer's schedule. Balancing the cost of my time against the cost of running the dryer, I come out better using the dryer.

Once the clothes are in the dryer, we often lose ourselves in other activities, knowing that the laundry will be there whenever we decide to return. This is a mistake. I arrange my schedule so that I'll be there the moment the dryer stops. Besides saving time, this also eliminates a lot of unnecessary ironing. I usually do this in the late afternoon when I'm home to greet the school buses. I'm occupying my hands but not my mind, so it's a good time to talk with a child. Folding the laundry doesn't require a high expenditure of emotional energy at "arsenic hour"—that time of day when your blood sugar has dropped, your energy has ebbed, and you'd like to slip someone a little arsenic or take a little yourself.

As you remove each garment from the clothesline or still-warm dryer, inspect it. Did it get clean? If not, what can you do about it? Plan for it. Does it need mending? If so, walk to the sewing machine (next to the laundry area) and do the job right then.

I used to just toss the torn garment on the machine,

and when I needed to use it or someone needed the garment, I would unearth the machine from under the pile and do the job on the spot while making someone late for something. Or I would say to myself, "I absolutely will not start this new sewing project until I've finished my mending," then I'd spend two hours of my precious-little sewing time catching up. This worked until the day I discovered my husband had seven pairs of undershorts awaiting repair and none to wear. Now I mend as I go and no longer get guilt feelings every time I walk by the sewing machine.

While I fold or hang the garments, I preheat the iron. The ironing board stays ready beside the dryer, the iron on it, and plugged in. I touch up the things that need it, turn off the iron, load the piles of clean clothes in a basket, and deliver them to their respective depositories.

Children can and should stash their own clothes. I put their clean, folded clothes on their beds, and from then on it's up to them. I do put my husband's clothes away—partly because I love him and try to spare him the nitty-gritty details when I can, and partly because I don't like the sight of their cluttering up our bed.

The total time I spend on clothing maintenance is about thirty minutes a day—five minutes to load the washer, fifteen to twenty minutes to fold, press, mend, and deliver. Three hours a week for laundry and mending isn't bad considering that the average city homemaker spends four hours and eighteen minutes on those jobs. It's the system that streamlines it.

No matter what system you develop, and you must find what works best for you, it all breaks down if you don't schedule it. That's what happened to my former mending habits. I didn't have a schedule. I did it when things got desperate. So—

HAVE A SCHEDULE

I know "Monday is washday" is a schedule all its own. But remember we're trying to eat a lot of elephants, and if you spend all day Monday on the wash elephant, you don't have the time or strength to tackle any others. I recommend segmenting laundry chores into manageable bits.

I divide our laundry into three color categories: whites, dark colors, and light colors. By doing one load of clothes each day I get by with six loads of wash—two of each color category—a week.

I facilitate the color coding by using only colored sheets for the master bedroom and rotating white and colored sheets for the other beds. Since I clean the master bedroom on Monday, I change the linen and do the light colored wash on that day. On Tuesday, I change the children's beds and do a white wash, including one set of white sheets. The colored linens from the other bed go in the hamper for the wash later in the week. On Wednesday, I do dark wash. Then I repeat the schedule the next three days—Thursday, light colors; Friday, whites; Saturday, dark colors. When my husband travels, I switch the Friday-Saturday schedule because I don't want to do the white wash on Friday, only to have him arrive home on Friday night with a suitcase full of dirty white shirts which he may need clean for another trip on Monday.

I also color code the towels. By assigning each child a specific color, I find: 1. Who's not bathing often enough; 2. Who's taking a clean towel each time they wash their hands; 3. Who drops the towels on the bathroom floor or puts them wet into the hamper to mold. Gone are the days of the "It wasn't me" protest.

Socks and shirts which come through the wash

wrong-side-out are returned to the wearer that way for him to turn or wear as he pleases. Our son turns his shirts but not the underwear or socks. In his words, "Nobody sees them. Besides, when I take them off they turn themselves so every other washing they're right-side-out."

Speaking of socks, I've found some little plastic discs which keep the socks together through the washing and drying process. I've given a supply of one color to my husband and a different color to our son. My husband clips his socks together before he puts them in the hamper. Our son may or may not. If not, I keep a supply of his discs in the bathroom and clip his socks as I remove them from the hamper. Oh, the joy of not staring at socks and trying to decide who they belong to. Oh, the time saved in not searching for the other sock. And because of the color coding, anyone can deliver the socks to their rightful owner. You could accomplish the same thing with safety pins—gold for one sock owner and silver for another. I know women who color code the socks by sewing a piece of colored thread in the toe, but that still doesn't keep the socks together.

Washing on schedule helps the children plan ahead on their wardrobe requirements. They can count on a dark wash on Wednesdays and know to get that favorite pair of jeans into the hamper the night before. Nothing "provokes a child to wrath" quite as quickly as not being able to wear a favorite outfit.

As soon as a wearer is old enough to choose what to wear, he's old enough to be responsible for it. What is in the hamper gets washed. Good old Mom shouldn't be a patsy, firing up the washer for one item. The rule is: If it's not clean you can: 1. wear something else; 2. wear it dirty (unless you're digging trenches it can't be that bad); 3. wash it out by hand. Having made the rule, it doesn't hurt to break it occasionally as long as the child understands that it's an act of love on my part, and not her inalienable right.

Having a schedule has given our home a modicum of peace. After all, the band uniform does have to be dry by Friday nights. Each of us bears the responsibility for anticipating our clothing needs and working their availability into the schedule. The schedule assures me that clothing maintained on a routine basis is more apt to be available. It also requires less expenditure of time and physical and emotional energy.

KEEP IT SIMPLE

Why maintain clothes that nobody wears? A closet or drawer full of seldom worn items makes you cram in the things you do wear, thereby creasing them so that they appear less-than-fresh. If you take the time to work out a system and a schedule for maintaining your clothes and linens, make sure you maintain only those which contribute to your way of life.

Go through your closets and drawers. About each garment, ask the question, "When was the last time somebody wore this?" If the answer is "more than a year ago," then chances are it won't ever be worn again. If you're sure that's the case, give the thing away. If you're in doubt, remove the garment from its present place. Store it in a spare closet or a box and date it. At the end of the year, if you still haven't used it, you probably won't. Get rid of it. If you can't bear to part with it, seal it in a dust-proof bag and relegate it to the attic, but don't keep reaching around it to get at something you do use. The same goes for seasonal clothes. Summer dresses have no business in your bed-room closet in December.

If your family members have some weird sense of their security being tied up with outgrown T-shirts and worn-out tennis shoes, welcome to the club. I don't have a good answer to the "but I might need it" syndrome, partly because I find I slide back into it my-self. Maybe you can talk them into the box idea. Maybe not. We all have our funny little foibles, and I never could be tyrant enough to discard without permission or insist that they discard—which explains why half of our extra closet holds twenty-year-old Air Force uni-forms and seventeen-year-old maternity dresses.

Once or twice a year, you could say, "Let's plan to analyze your wardrobe this week and see what needs replacing." The promise of replacement (something new "instead of," not "in addition to") sometimes pro-vides the impetus to part with a few cherished rags. You'll have to set the example here by ridding your dresser drawers of the lingerie with stretched-out elas-tic, the high school era sweaters (yes, even if they're cashmere), and the mistakes you bought when you were in a hurry.

Sometimes, more-desperate measures are in order. Our teenage son has a thing about T-shirts with de-signs on them. At last count, he had twenty-seven. Count them, twenty-seven. Some he's had so long that he'd strangle if he tried to put them on. When the struggle to put anything in his dresser drawers re-quired both my hands and one foot, I instituted the rule of each child putting his own clothes away. The first night he went to bed and had to remove four stacks of clean clothes before he could lie down. He yelled, "That's a dirty trick!" Then he transferred them to the spare bed, from which he uses them as he needs them. Unsightly? You bet. I just keep his bedroom door closed. When it bothers him enough, he'll do something about it. Meanwhile, I've chosen to do something more worthwhile with my time than wrestle with his T-shirts.

In Chapter 4, I recommend asking the question, "Could someone else do this task as well or better?" Clothing maintenance is another area where we can answer yes, and should, not only in the interest of saving time, but also in training our children in self-sufficiency.

Systematize your operation. Schedule your wash days. Simplify by eliminating the unnecessary. And get help.

7 Eating Eats Time— Buying Food

Probably nothing about housework takes as much time, energy, and thought as cooking. And no task leaves less to show for it. Do the laundry and the linen closet shelves reveal stacks of fresh-smelling, neatly folded sheets and towels. Clean the house and the rug stays unlittered for a couple of hours. But prepare a meal and thirty minutes later you have only dirty dishes.

There are people who fulfill their creative urges in the kitchen. Some people even earn their living cooking. Others exist on a diet of quick dinners that taste like aluminum foil. They know the location of every fast food joint within twenty miles. I'm somewhere in between. I like to eat good food. I don't mind cooking it. But God has other things for me to do, so I try to do the best job in the least amount of time. Once again I use the three time savers—system, schedule, and simplification.

Time management expert Lillian Gilbreth, in her book *Management in the Home,* says that all jobs have three parts—get ready, do, and clean up. We could describe the feeding of a family in these three parts. Get ready—menu planning and purchasing of food. Do—cook and serve. Clean up—well, clean up. Obviously we go down this road a lot further. We subdivide the get ready step into its own three steps of: 1. Get ready—read newspaper grocery ads for specials, consult calendar of activities and plan menus, and make up shopping list; 2. Do—purchase groceries; 3. Clean up—put away groceries. This chapter and the two following deal with ways to systematize, schedule, and simplify these steps.

GET READY TO FOOD SHOP

Systematize your planning. Keep a pad and pencil handy in the kitchen to note supplies which need replenishing. This running list becomes your shopping agenda for the week. Jot down any advertised specials that budget and space will permit you to stockpile.

Consult your planning calendar for the week's activities. Who will be eating what meals where? Now make a menu chart like the one in Figure 1.

Consult your freezer and pantry inventory lists. Plan to use what you already have in stock before buying anything else—other than the specials. Write down the complete meal. For example, Breakfast: orange juice, sausage, pancakes, butter, syrup, coffee, milk. If you don't write it down, you may find after mixing the pancake batter that the syrup bottle is almost empty—something you should have caught and put on your running list the last time you used it.

After planning the week's menus, think about the ingredients you'll need to prepare each dish. Check to see if you have them, and list those you'll need to buy. When using a new or seldom-prepared recipe, look it up and jot down quantities to purchase. Post the menu on your kitchen bulletin board.

WEEKLY MENUS

Day	Breakfast	Lunch	Dinner
Wednesday			
Thursday			
Friday			

Figure 1.

Analyze your shopping list and group like items. I hate to recopy a list, so I letter-code mine by category. That way, when I get to a certain section of the supermarket I can spot the items on my list (see Figure 2). At the canned fruit shelf I look for all the "E" items, in the dairy case the "D" coded foods, etc.

If you know your market well enough, you might code by aisles. My market keeps rearranging things, and I don't always shop at the same store. But most markets do keep like items reasonably together.

GROCERY LIST

A Lettuce B Dishwasher detergent	E Applesauce	C Grape juice E Pineapple chunks
C Apple juice D Cheese	A Cantaloupe	D Eggs

Figure 2.

The next time your children need a rainy day activity, have them take a blank tablet and divide each page into eight sections. Label the sections Dairy, Meat, Produce, Canned Goods, Bakery, Frozen Foods, Condiments, and Cleaning Supplies. Use this tablet for your grocery list and you'll be way ahead. (Now why didn't I think of that while my children were young enough to think it was fun?)

Do Your Shopping

The less often we have to food shop, the less time it will take. I have a friend who food shops once a month for her family of six. It takes her about three hours and lots of energy. Few of us have sufficient storage space for that many provisions, but unless we live without refrigeration we should be able to get by with a once-a-week foray. If we spend an hour to an hour and a half at our shopping, we've still saved time over the cook who goes out every day, because there's no way she can do it in less than thirty minutes a trip. Food shopping is one elephant that we don't want to chop into tiny bites. If we have a place to store it, we should buy the whole elephant.

You can save some time by shopping when most other people don't. I know a woman who does her marketing on Saturday night. I've found that dinner hour is a good time to shop, because everyone else is home, cooking. Working wives, I've also found that stopping at the store on the way home from work is a disaster, because every other working person is doing the same thing. Besides, you're hungry and apt to buy things you don't need.

My schedule has an hour between dinner and prayer meeting on Wednesday nights, and since I'm just a half mile from the supermarket, I shop then. When checking out, I pack all refrigerated and frozen foods together. Then I transfer them to an old styrofoam cooler I keep in the trunk of the car. That way, I can go to prayer meeting without worrying about a thaw.

When you shop, discipline yourself to move quickly through the store, buying only what's on your list. Try to keep like items together in your cart. You can facilitate your unpacking and putting away and win the gratitude of the busy cashier by sacking your own groceries. I actually look for a checkout stand with no bag boy. I open about five sacks, and as the checker pushes the groceries at me, I sort and bag them according to where I want to store them at home. One bag gets all the deep freeze foods, the laundry supplies, and the produce to be stored in the cool basement. When I get home I don't have to carry those items upstairs, sort them, and carry them back down again. Another bag holds the pantry items, and a third holds things destined for the refrigerator.

STASH IT

So you've bought your groceries and lugged them home. If you've bagged them yourself, you can take each bag directly to the appropriate storage area. If not, there they sit on the kitchen table—mysterious brown bags. You have no idea what each one contains.

Put one sack on a chair so you can reach into it easily. Using both hands, remove items and place them on the kitchen table, sorting them by storage area. After you've unpacked and sorted all the bags, walk one time to the freezer, mark your inventory, open the door, and stash all items that belong there. If your table is too far removed from storage areas, sort onto trays, or back into bags, but move, all-at-one-time, all items destined for the same place.

Today's home has basically three storage areas—freezer, refrigerator, and cupboards or pantry. Your system for storing your provisions can add to or cut your preparation time. Let's look at the areas and ask the "why" questions.

Deep Freezer—why use it? For preservation of food. That's straightforward enough, and we don't find ourselves storing nonperishables in the deep freezer. We can save precious minutes (not to mention money when we stand there with the door open) by knowing what we have in the freezer and where to find it. I recommend an inventory sheet and a pencil on a string taped to the freezer door. List the freezer inventory by shelf (and expiration date if of limited storage time), grouping like items together. For example: "Bottom shelf—meat. 1 pot roast, 3 pkgs. hamburger patties, 1 turkey breast," etc.

Form the habit of faithfully logging new items onto the inventory and crossing off those used. Train other family members to do the same. Gone forever are the times of frostbitten fingers digging through hoary packages of something that may have been broccoli at one time, while you look for that can of orange juice you could have sworn you had. You also speed up your menu planning by knowing what's on hand.

Your first inventory will be the hardest to make up and may shock you when you find a mummified angel food cake underneath the homegrown squash, but do it. After you've designed the first inventory form, someone else can make copies. Like someone who comes to you and says, "Mom, I don't have anything to do."

Refrigerator—why use it? To retard spoilage and to improve the flavor of certain items by chilling. If that's true, why are you storing, reaching around, and moving food items that needn't be refrigerated—like mustard, worcestershire, or soy sauce? Since you have to keep cleaning the refrigerator, keep in it only those things that need refrigeration.

Since the turnover of refrigerated foods is pretty high, I don't recommend an inventory for it. If you're cleaning your refrigerator one shelf every morning as you do the breakfast cleanup, you know what's in it. However, a list for the freezer portion of the refrigerator may help you. It also lets the children see what snacks they can have.

Pantry and cupboards—why do we put certain items in certain places? For convenience, I hope. Divide your storage for non-perishables into two categories: the often-used and the stockpiled.

Your stockpile includes items like the soup you found on special, five cans for a dollar; the extra roll of paper towel you bought because the present roll was getting thin; the gallon jug of vinegar from which you fill the serving cruet. In other words, the items you don't use often.

To eliminate search time and streamline menu planning, keep an inventory of the pantry area, just as you do the deep freeze. Again, group like items and keep the list current. Use a separate sheet of paper for each shelf to avoid recopying the entire inventory when you use the food on one shelf faster than that on the others. Your shelf lists will not only help you systematize your storage, but they will also help you simplify by calling attention to the food that you've had in the pantry too long. After you've written down that can of carob powder enough times, you'll either use it or pitch it.

Keep the often-used foods close to where they'll be used. Even I balk at storing the peanut butter and jelly on the kitchen table, but how about near the breadbox and the table knives? And why store the table salt over the sink when you never salt anything in the sink? Devise your own storage, but continually ask, "Why in that place? Do I use it most often there?" You won't need an inventory of high-use items, because you use them often enough to know when they're running low.

Like most time-saving techniques, the first times you purchase your food this way, you'll feel it's slow and awkward. Keep at it. Soon you'll make it a habit and once again prove the law of economy of efficiency—do something often enough and you'll learn to do it better, faster. The careful control of your purchasing system will save you time in preparation, too.

8 Eating Eats Time— Preparing and Serving Food

Food preparation has its own set of get ready, do, and clean up. Since I'm not writing a cookbook or a nutrition manual, I shall refrain from describing how you can serve one pound of ground beef for three meals. Instead, I'll stick to time-control tips.

One of your biggest time savers is still doubling recipes and freezing half—provided you find it in the freezer and use it before it loses its identity. The other time savers are (you guessed it) your schedule, your system, and simplicity.

THE SCHEDULE

Mealtimes dictate the schedule. Most of us eat three meals a day, and the rest of our daily schedules revolve around these fixed (more or less) times. You may live alone and exist on a diet of tinned sardines, boiled eggs, and canned biscuits. You may be chief cook and bottle washer for a crew of starving farmhands or teenagers (the difference being that teenagers generally complain more). Or maybe you have someone else doing the cooking, and all you have to do is show up at the table. In any case, the consumption of food (and its preparation) requires time. It is a fixed item in your time budget. Accept it. Allow for it. But don't let it have more than its rightful share.

Lillian Gilbreth suggests that whenever possible, try to combine the cleanup step of one job with the get ready step of another. Thus, you begin preparation of the next day's meals while you do the after-dinner cleanup. Here's where the schedule and the system mesh. The way you do it dictates when you do it.

After dinner, load the dishwasher and turn it on, or hand wash the dishes and let them drain. Look over the breakfast menu. Does orange juice need thawing? Transfer it from freezer to refrigerator. Section the grapefruit or cut up the melon, and cover it with plastic wrap. Put water and coffee in the coffee maker, and plug it into an automatic outlet timer. You can buy one at the hardware store for about five dollars. It pays for itself the first morning you stumble bleary-eyed into the kitchen and smell the freshly brewed coffee awaiting you. Complete any other preparations you can. Cook sausage or bacon the night before, and wrap it in foil for a quick heat-up in the morning. Beat the eggs for scrambling. Mix the pancake or waffle batter.

Now look at the lunch and dinner menus. Will you be too rushed in the morning to think about thawing meat or bread? Transfer from freezer to refrigerator now. Dinner plans call for gelatin salad? Make it now. Wash and drain salad greens, wrap them in paper towel, and return them to the crisper drawer. Perform these operations while you're cleaning up the kitchen. Don't even return place mats and napkins to the drawer. Leave them on the table. It doesn't look messy. It looks ready for the next meal. By this time the dishwasher should have finished doing its thing. Empty the dishwasher or drainer, setting the table for the next meal as you do. This way you're ready for the next batch of dirty dishes, and you've saved yourself the time and energy of handling the clean ones twice.

THE SYSTEM

When preparing a dish, read the recipe all the way through. Collect all ingredients and equipment before you begin. Use a tray. Open the refrigerator and pantry doors once, and get everything you need. When cleaning up afterward, reverse the process. If you are an experienced cook, you know to preheat the oven and grease the pans before you begin to assemble your concoction. Sounds simple, doesn't it? But you and I know the organization and sense of timing it takes to bring five different dishes, all requiring different preparation methods and cooking times, to the table on schedule. It takes planning.

Remember the chapter on planning? Step 4 says "Establish starting time." Start with the time you want the meal on the table. Note the cooking and preparation time for each dish, and establish a starting time for each operation. If starting times overlap, something has to give. Much of the time we establish these starting times in our heads—it's second nature to us. However, when planning a Christmas feast, cooking an unfamiliar dish, or aiming for an exact serving time, it's best to write it all down.

Two tricks I've learned about serving a meal save much confusion at the last minute. One comes from the experience of working as a waitress. That is, put all cold items on the table (water, butter, jam, salad, condiments) before serving the hot food. You can usually find a lull during preparation time to do this.

The other trick evolved out of my frustration at slaving over a meal and putting it on the table, only to have it grow cold while diners straggled in one at a time. My husband's family was especially bad about this. They'd look in the dining room, see no food on the table, and resume their activities even though I'd called them to eat. Meanwhile, I'd be in the kitchen, muttering, "The diner should wait upon the food and never the food upon the diner." Now, I serve a first course of juice, soup, or salad which I put on the table for all to see. I leave the hot food on the stove to serve while they're waiting for it. Not to be sacrilegious, but this helps greatly, too, when someone waxes too eloquent over the blessing.

We all have our favorite tricks. I'm sure you could tell me at least as many as I'm telling you. And I'd like to hear them. After all, that's what made Heloise famous. Here are a few more of mine:

Measure dry ingredients first so you can use the same measuring tools for wet ingredients.

Cook a big roast. Thin-slice the remainder with an electric knife, and put it in sandwich buns. Wrap individual sandwiches in foil and freeze. To serve, heat at 350° for fifteen minutes.

Cook bulk sausage in the roll. Remove wrapper. Bake sausage in a plastic roasting bag (follow directions for use of the bag) at 350° for one hour. Drain on paper towels and cool. Slice. Wrap in foil and refrigerate. To heat, place foil package in oven or frying pan.

Cook bacon ahead by baking it on a rack in a shallow pan at 400° until crisp (about twenty minutes). Wrap it in foil and reheat as with sausage.

For potato salad, boil potatoes and eggs together in the same pan.

Make extra waffle or pancake batter. Cook until

done but not browned. Freeze for later browning in toaster or oven. Freeze leftover french toast for the same treatment.

Split leftover muffins and biscuits for freezing. Wrapped in foil, they thaw and heat through in about six to eight minutes at 400°.

Save used foil trays and make your own TV dinners with leftovers. Freeze them for a busy night.

Use a crockpot for roasting beef, pork, or chicken. Saves splattering in the oven and cooks while you're gone.

Cook turkey on days other than Thanksgiving and Christmas. Slice as much as you can and freeze it for sandwiches. Cut up the carcass and simmer it in water overnight in a covered kettle. Freeze the meat bits for later use in turkey pie or turkey salad. Cool the broth to harden the fat. Discard the fat and freeze the broth for soups.

Most of the efficiencies we practice come as a result of our asking ourselves, "Why do I _____?" or "Why can't I _____?" As you establish your own system and schedule for preparing and serving food, continue to ask these questions.

9 Eating Makes a Mess

A working kitchen, one producing lovin' from the oven, gets dirty. The tools get dirty. The counter and cooking surfaces get sticky. The floor gets crumby. The washing of cooking utensils makes up just one part of the total cleanup job.

Someone once said that dust removed often is just dust. But dust allowed to combine with the moisture in the air becomes grime and takes twice as much time and effort to remove. In the kitchen, the problem is compounded by the minute grease particles which combine with the moisture and dust to produce something my family calls crud. This is the other kitchen cleanup which takes less time if done routinely and often.

We can eliminate much of the drudgery of kitchen cleanup by not letting it pile up on us. One bite at a time, right? That means a schedule. And we can save precious seconds by cutting down on search, fetch, and put-back time. That calls for a good hard look at the system.

Streamline Your Storage

Let's look, first, at the inevitable wash up and put away that accompanies food preparation and consumption. I've already recommended storing foods at the point where they're most often used. Let's apply this rule to the equipment used in preparing and serving the food. Store your tools where you use them. What has this to do with cleaning up the kitchen and getting out of it fast? Two things.

First, once you establish a sensible storage point for an item, train yourself and others to always return the item to its assigned spot. You can slip into habitual, rhythmic motions of putting things away without giving them a lot of think time. Second, you eliminate search-for time the next time you need the tool. You cut down on fetch time by storing it where you use it instead of several steps away.

Have a storage system. Think it through. Try it out. If it doesn't work, change it. Make two firm rules for your kitchen:

1. I will store things that I use often at the point where I will use them.

2. I will avoid bending, or stretching, or moving other objects to get at or put back the items I use most often.

If you have always thrived on grouping like things together, you may experience some trauma when you separate the glasses you use every day from the six dozen other glasses for special occasions. Put everyday glasses with everyday dishes, next to the table where you'll use them and close to the dishwashing center. Do this with flatwear, china, and serving pieces. If you have to, ask yourself why you should store all the glasses together. And who said so? It gets back to the question of who's in charge of your kitchen.

While you're working out an efficient storage system for your tools, go ahead and simplify at the same time. Get a box and mark it "Seldom-Used Kitchen Tools." Now get a bigger box. Mark it "Flea Market." Into the flea market box put all the unworkable gadgets you bought on impulse, all the impractical gifts, the extra pieces bought when you couldn't find the one you already had—all the tools you never use. Donate this box to some charitable organization or save it for your next garage sale, when your junk will become someone else's junk.

Put the tools you use occasionally—the Christmas cookie cutters, the skewers for trussing the Thanksgiving turkey, the twice-a-year or less items—into your "Seldom-Used" box, and put the box in the attic, the basement, the garage, or somewhere where you won't have to move it to clean or get at something else.

Shift and rearrange what's left until you've arrived at a workable system. Keep asking why? Why do you keep the wire whisk in a drawer across the kitchen from the mixing bowls? When was the last time you whisked anything without a bowl?

WHY HANDLE THINGS TWICE?

Having finally arrived at a place for everything, aim at getting everything back to its place as soon as possible. I don't mean stand there and wait for the dishwasher to stop or dry pots when they could just as well air dry in the dish drainer. I do mean, get a tool as far along in the process of getting back to its assigned spot as is practical. When you empty a bowl, squirt a little dishwashing liquid in it, put it in the sink, and fill it with water. Drop smaller utensils into it. As soon as you have a break in the action, wash that batch and let them drain. When dishing up a meal, wash each pan as you empty it. After eating you'll only need to wash the eating utensils and wipe the counter tops and range.

If you need to transport more than two tools more than two or three steps, use a tray. Handle an item only once. Clear the table directly to the dishwasher instead of to the counter and then to the dishwasher. If you have no dishwasher, scrape, rinse, and stack before you serve up dessert. When clearing, washing, and stacking, train yourself to pick up items with both hands instead of picking up with the left hand, transferring to the right hand, and from there to the cupboard.

When emptying the dishwasher or drainer, use the dishes to re-set the table for the next meal instead of putting the dishes in the cupboard. Do this before you begin preparation for the next meal in order to have the dishwasher empty for the next batch of cooking tools. Besides eliminating double handling, I've found there's a great psychological benefit in having the table set. Hungry people can see at least the promise of something happening.

KEEP ONE STEP AHEAD

That takes care of the every-meal mess. What about the appliances and surfaces that gather dust, spatters, and finger marks? That's where the old schedule comes in. You want to get to that dirt before it becomes crud or a health hazard, but you don't want to clean items which do not need cleaning. Plan for it. Ask why. Make a schedule.

I prefer to keep after things. Each morning while doing the breakfast cleanup I clean one refrigerator shelf. It takes me about two minutes to remove the contents of the shelf (I either plan my lunch around the leftovers or pitch them out), wash the shelf, and replace the contents. That way my refrigerator has a complete going-over every ten days or so.

I also clean one drawer or shelf or countertop and one range burner every morning. Again, it takes about two minutes each. I move counterclockwise around the kitchen, and it takes about six months to get all the cupboards and surfaces. Then I start over.

The time to clean the oven is when it gets spattered, not after the blueberries have baked into the enamel. During after-dinner clean up, pour pure ammonia into a sauce dish and set it in the oven. Plug up the vent with paper towels. Next morning, put on rubber gloves, turn on the exhaust fan, hold your breath, remove the paper towel plug, open the oven door, and step back for a few moments. Take off your rings and let them soak in the dish of ammonia while you wash oven surfaces with a wet sponge or cloth. (Oh yes, somewhere in there, start breathing again.) The grease floats off. I don't know why. Swish the rings around in the ammonia, rinse them, and dry with a soft cloth. Discard the ammonia. If the oven doesn't all come clean, repeat the process the next night. Sometimes the grime goes on in layers and has to come off the same way.

Tom Sawyer Tactics

In these three chapters on eating, I haven't said much about getting help. A lot of women prefer solitude in the kitchen. Yet, helpers can save you precious time. The trick is to train, and let your helpers do the jobs they enjoy. Our daughter likes to bake—so I let her. She doesn't do such a hot job cleaning up afterward, but if I had to bake and clean up too, I'd have even less time. My husband seems to enjoy scrubbing pots to a high shine, and I wouldn't spoil his fun for anything. He scrubs while I put the food away. Our helpers are reluctant because too often we give them the jobs we don't want to do.

Systematize your every-meal cleanup and eliminate unnecessary movements. Schedule routine cleaning of all kitchen surfaces. And get help. Children can set a table, load and unload a dishwasher, or use a bottle of spray cleaner and paper towels. They even think it's fun.

10 Working Women, Read This First

My apologies to those of you who slave all day at home yet are never referred to as working women. We know better. But "working wives" has become a convenient euphemism for differentiating between those who get paid in dollars for their work and those who don't. Those of us who've had it both ways wonder who to pity and who really gets the better reward. But. . . .

If you're one of the millions of women employed outside your home and you didn't read this chapter first, you're probably shaking your head and saying, "Yes, but. . . ."

And I don't blame you. Read on. I do understand.

As I finished drafting this section of the book, I had the uneasy feeling that it didn't speak to the problems of the woman who works at another job all day and then comes home and has to pack all of her housework into the remaining time and ebbing energy. I tried to think how it was. The best I could do was to remember coming home from work one winter night—dog-tired, bone-weary, heavy with child, and my husband's bringing me a pair of flat-heeled shoes and saying, "Here. Wear these while you cook dinner."

Somehow, seventeen years of being your own boss

dims the most unpleasant of the memories. I began to ask myself how I could write a book for all women when I couldn't remember the problems of all women. But God's hand has been on the writing of this book, for He provided the opportunity for me to become an employed wife again.

The details aren't important. Through prayer, the laying down of a fleece, and the encouragement of my family, I believed God had led me to the job. I invested a little money in a ladylike wardrobe (when you've lived for seventeen years in blue jeans, you're not exactly equipped to present a professional appearance) and began doing the eight-to-five bit.

Within a month of my joining the labor force, I had also joined the chorus of women who said, "It sure is hard to have time for anything when you work."

Houseplants withered and died. The cat refused to use her litter pan because it was full of litter. The laundry piled up. So did the mending. Bills that should have been paid got lost in the pile of papers on my desk. The children, proud of their "professional" mother, wanted the money I earned, but also wanted the services I'd provided before. My dear husband, also proud of me, kept saying, "You realize you'll have to give up some of your other activities, . . ." then went right on expecting me to take part in his. Inevitably, conflicts arose.

I refused to sacrifice my morning quiet hour. Since I had to be in the kitchen, completely dressed and painted, by 7:00 A.M. and my ritual (including shower, shampoo, and blow dry) takes forty-five minutes, I had to get up at 5:00 A.M. No problem—I'm a morning person. No problem, that is, until bedtime. We'd crawl into bed, my husband ready for love, and I ready for sleep. He felt rejected. I felt guilty.

I began to spread at the hips. The morning schedule allowed no time for exercise. I sat at a desk all day. By bedtime, I couldn't face the thought of forcing my weary body to go through an exercise routine. Lots of nights I went to bed with my makeup on, too tired to wash my face. My skin began to look old.

As I was about to go under for the third time, wondering how I could have misread God's will so badly, a quiet voice said, "Go back to the basics."

I asked, "What basics? What do you mean, Lord?"

And He answered, "Just what you've been writing about. Do you believe in what you've written or don't you? Either the principles work or they don't."

"Of course I believe them. I wouldn't write what I don't believe. They worked for me."

"Then when are you going to start practicing them again?" He persisted.

Brought up short that way, I had to admit that all my beautiful organization—system, schedule, and simplicity—was in imminent danger of collapse. Why? Because after teaching and writing that it takes time to get organized and you have to spend time to save time, I had allowed my employment to push me into a corner where I hadn't taken the time myself. Thus, chagrined, I went back to the basics. It went something like this.

ATTITUDE

I chose to go to work, therefore I choose to spend my time in a certain manner—no one controls this but me. I caught myself a time or two justifying my working on the basis of a son about ready for college and costs so high. But I knew better. We could have chosen a simpler lifestyle. We could have taken out a loan. The "But I have to work" was a lie. I worked because I wanted to. At the scent of a challenge, my ego had reared its ugly head and said, "Sic 'em."

Then why all these apologetic, self-pitying feelings? Stark reality dictated that I could not put ten pounds in a five pound bag. I had to give up many activities. Some of them (professional meetings, my Christian writers group, the Shakespeare club), although I missed them, had been for my own pleasure and did not engender guilt feelings. But the volunteer work, the church choirs, the speaking and teaching engagements, the sewing, the gardening—the activities through which I served other people—also had to go. And that hurt, for through these activities I had let God's love flow to others. And this was where I was most tempted (and still am) to justify my employment on the basis of something other than my own desire. I have to continually reestablish in my mind that I work by choice and cannot expect others to pay for it.

To my employed sisters everywhere, let me remind you not to expect understanding from those who choose to stay at home. I write as one who knows. They have little sympathy for those of us who work by choice. They don't like to hear us whining, "But I work." They get tired of providing services to our children and carrying a double load in church and community. And who can blame them? We must never forget that we work by choice and that as we do, we also choose to give up certain freedoms. We must not expect that just because we work someone is obligated to take up the slack where we've dropped out. We should make our own arrangements for getting things done. In some cases it will cost us dearly, but that's part of the price of employment.

For those women who have no choice but to work—the singles, those with one-parent homes or disabled husbands, and the many whose husband's income can't support a family—I have a greater compassion now. Many of you can legitimately say, "But I have to work." I hope the contents of this book will help you in the better use of the rest of your time.

PRIORITIES AND GOALS

I asked myself again, "What are my priorities? On what will I not compromise?" That was the first step to getting it all straight again, for I had to answer:

1. I will not compromise my relationship with God. He and I have come too far together, and I know too much now about my dependence on Him to ever go back to trying to live my life alone. Therefore, my time with Him will be inviolable.

2. I will not compromise my relationship with my family. We have a good marriage because my husband and I both work at it. Therefore, I will try to be attractive and available to my husband and our children.

3. I believe that God's mission for me right now is to help other women realize their potential in Him. He has called me to write this book for that purpose. This will be my third priority.

4. Because I can no longer give a lot of time to volunteer projects, I must love people into the kingdom of heaven wherever I happen to find them—lifestyle evangelism.

My goals didn't change when I began working, though I had to greatly extend the time allotted to achieve each of them. I had to satisfy myself with much smaller bites on the elephant.

PLANNING

Not only did planning become more vital, but I also had to plan times to sit down and plan. Although the systems I'd devised were good, sound systems, I had to completely revamp my lovely schedule. After living for one month with no intermediate- and short-range plans, I was missing deadlines, forgetting appointments, offending people, acting scatterbrained, and living from one weekend to the next.

Another look at the basics made me ask again the four questions of Chapter 3:

1. Is there a faster way? Probably. But I must take the time to think out the faster way. I had to get over the idea that plunging in and kicking up a lot of dust accomplished anything. Think time became as important as do time.

2. Does this task need doing? Suddenly, having everything vacuumed, dusted, and scrubbed twice a week seemed silly. As long as we weren't inundated with bugs and the county health officer wasn't knocking at our door, who cared about a few crumbs under the table? Only the cat and I. No wonder my family never went into raptures about how clean I kept the house. They don't notice the dirt!

3. Could someone else do it as well or better? Definitely. I offered the maid more money for more hours of work, and she happily obliged. I assigned a payment value to household chores, and our daughter was glad to earn a little extra by doing them. I didn't nag. If she got to the job and did it before I could get to it, she got paid. Otherwise she didn't.

I no longer felt apologetic about asking for help because I no longer had any more time than anyone else. Our son has run many errands and helped out with my

Christmas shopping. Whenever possible, I let someone else drive while I make up menus, write letters, or close my eyes and rest. When my wonderful mother-in-law asked how she could help, I suggested the mending. She has happily and beautifully kept us from coming apart at the seams. My husband took over supervision of school work, teacher conferences, and much of the band booster work.

4. Can it be postponed? Not always. Christmas comes on schedule, and you either shop, decorate, and bake or you don't. Even that elephant can be tackled a little at a time. Each evening, as I cooked dinner, I mixed up a batch of dough for our traditional cookies and breads. I refrigerated them all, and then on one night I had a baking orgy. I can put off until Saturday, when I have a fresh supply of energy, many of the chores I had tried to do in the evenings. And I can put off until after Christmas some of the chores I would normally do in December.

I'm managing to survive by utilizing the fragments of time to eat a lot of elephants. Here's how.

I still roll out at 5:00 A.M. for my quiet time and breakfast. I figure God would rather have me study His Word over coffee and cheese toast than not at all. Having started the day with God and having committed it to Him, I expect Him to help me get it all together.

I glance over the day's schedule. (I've had to start making the schedule the night before. There's no time in the morning, and if I wait until I get home from work to do it, I'm so mentally tired that I find it hard to think of working. But if I've already written it down and apportioned out the time, I'm more apt to carry through.) Then it's to the shower, and here's where doing things the night before begins to count.

By checking clothing needs and making breakfast preparations the night before, I can serve a good breakfast, make the bed, and get out the door on time, looking reasonably sharp and in a good mood. I'm grateful that God helped streamline our housekeeping operations before He sent me out to work. The system, the inventories, the efficient movements have made the difference between merely surviving and having things under control.

Lunch hour affords enough time for one or two errands. By taking a thermos of liquid lunch (try one cup of milk, one egg, two tablespoons of protein powder, one teaspoon of lecithin, and one-half a banana all whirred in the blender) I can drink and drive—to the bank, the post office, the store. I've successfully completed all our Christmas shopping and mailing this way. I've found a dry cleaner who opens at 6:00 A.M., and by leaving for work five minutes early I can get that stop out of the way.

Late in the afternoon, I phone our daughter. We chat about her day, and I give her instructions for starting dinner. Unless other stops along the way are absolutely necessary, I go home immediately after work.

As soon as I've greeted everyone, I gather up the laundry for the day and start the washer. Then I cook. Dinner is our family time, and I try to keep it pleasant and unhurried. After dinner, I transfer laundry to dryer and we clean up the kitchen together. The cleaning of refrigerator, range, and cupboards, which I used to do in the morning during my peaceful pre-employment days, I've moved to evening. This leaves me three hours in which to pack ten hours worth of work.

Sometimes, if I've had a rough day, I take a thirty-minute nap. Right now, with the writing schedule so tight, I spend more time at the typewriter and less elsewhere. Whatever I'm doing, I keep an ear open for the dryer's stopping so that I can snatch out the clothes.

It's taken me a while, but I've finally worked out an exercise schedule. At work, I run up and down a flight of stairs for five minutes each morning and afternoon. On days when I don't run errands during lunch break, I put on walking shoes and take a thirty-minute walk. I schedule the last thirty minutes before bedtime for self-improvement. This includes exercises, skin, teeth, and nail care. The trick is to write it into the schedule and not to wait until so late in the evening that I'm too tired to do it.

It has not all been sweetness and light, and I don't have it all tacked down yet. I've had to resign myself to giving up some really pleasurable activities. But I have also sloughed off some time wasters (by the way, they didn't seem like wasters until I had no time for them). I've found that my God does supply all my needs, and along with Judith Miles, author of *The Feminine Principle*, I can say, "Our time, like our money, is eaten up with non-essentials without God's hand on us."

Like someone who has found she has only a short time to live, I have found that important things grow more important, and other things, which lack eternal value, fade into insignificance. That's my choice at this moment.

11 Time for Me

Most women want to look good. Their egos, sense of well-being, confidence, femininity, and sexuality are all tied up in how they think they look. But God's woman looks at appearance from a different perspective. Of course she wants to look, smell, and sound her very best. After all, she is an ambassador for the King. But her physical beauty is never an end in itself. She knows that her attractiveness draws people to her. And in drawing close, they are blessed by the richness of her life.

Some women are born beautiful. The rest of us have to work at it. The older we get, the more time it takes. But we must take that time. And we need to strike a balance between too much time and not enough.

I don't qualify to write a book on beauty or even on physical culture. I write to encourage you to look at what you are doing now. See if there is a way you can get good results in less time. Let's start at the top with your hair and work down through makeup, figure, clothes, and good health.

YOUR CROWNING GLORY

If you can afford the time and money for a professional hairdresser once or twice a week, go to it. Just be sure you plan to use your time twice by taking some sort of hand work (letter writing, menu planning, mending) to do while you wait.

I've decided that those weekly trips are meant for women with more time and money than I. My metabolism and my need to look well-put-together for my work dictate a daily shampoo. With the aid of a blow dryer and an electric curling iron, I manage to keep my hair attractive. To do this I get a good basic cut appropriate to my face shape, my age, my overall size, and my lifestyle. I have the stylist show me how to maintain the style. Then I have my hair trimmed often enough (every four to six weeks) to keep the basic shape.

Analyze your day. What time makes best sense for your hair care? Mornings before you start out for work? Afternoons while the baby naps? Schedule it.

Do you have a system? Ask yourself why you do things a certain way. If you shampoo in the shower, why keep your shampoo in the linen closet? If you blow dry every day, why unplug the dryer and put it in a drawer? Apply the same time-saving techniques to hair care that you do to house care.

YOUR MAKEUP

The beauty experts tell us that having a routine is far more important than what the routine is. Even the most skilled makeup artist can't completely camouflage the ravages of neglected skin. Consistent skin care pays off whether you use famous-name products or get them from a five-and-ten cent store. Read a book, have a consultation, do whatever you need to do to find what's right for your skin; then stick with it.

Decide how often you need to go through your routine and schedule it. If you've allowed time for it, you're less likely to skip it when you're tired or hurried. Schedule the occasional facials and tweezings, too.

Establish a system and do the same things the same way each time. Pretty soon habit will take over and free your mind for other thoughts.

Because I dislike clutter, I keep my makeup in a zippered case. As part of my system, as I remove items from the case, I line them up in the order I'll use them. It takes no extra time, yet it saves "search for" time.

Just as you organized your kitchen cupboards, you must streamline your cosmetic case. Keep all your cleaning and cosmetic supplies in the place where you'll use them. Get rid of what you're not using so that you don't have to dust it or reach around it to get what you want. If you can afford it, buy duplicates of the makeup items you like to carry in your purse. Keep one set at home with your basic supplies to eliminate digging through your purse every morning to find mascara and lipstick. Keep on asking yourself, why here? Why now? Why this way?

YOUR CLOTHING

I've written a whole chapter on clothing maintenance, but I want to say more here about looking better in what you wear while spending less time at it.

What most of us need in the clothing line is not more of everything. We need to look well-put-together in a few good outfits, then wear them often enough to get our money's worth out of them.

First, find your color group. Do you look good in golden tones? Or do you look best in the pale, icy colors? Maybe the vivid tones become you best. By the way, it has nothing to do with hair color or sun tan or the color you like best (you may like to look at that color but look horrid in it). Your ideal color grouping has to do with your underlying skin tones. Why do I make so much of this? Because it can save you time and a bundle of money.

To help you decide which colors become you best, get a group of friends together (friends who will tell you the truth) and constructively criticize each other. Collect as many different solid-colored fabrics as you can get your hands on. The fabric pieces will need to be about twelve inches by twenty-four inches—big enough to drape around your neck. Separate the pieces into color groups. Drape around your neck all the different shades of a color, one after another, and let your friends choose the shades which make your face and eyes come alive. Lay these pieces aside. Then go on to the next color.

When you have tried all the shades and chosen one or more of each color, you'll find that "your" colors fall into a certain category—gold tones, icy tones, vivid tones, or clear tones. You'll sparkle in that color grouping. Take advantage of it. Cut two-inch swatches of the fabrics in that color group. You could have as many as twenty-five or thirty different swatches. Insert them into a clear plastic credit card holder which you can carry with you at all times.

Build your wardrobe around your colors. Of course you can't scrap perfectly good clothing, but as you replace items, always buy in your color group. Over a period of time you'll accumulate clothing and accessories that do the most for you.

Now here is the best part. You save time and money by eliminating costly mistakes—you know, the ones you buy and never wear. You'll also save time in accessorizing outfits, because all your shoes, purses, scarves, and jewelry will fit with all the colors in your grouping. You'll solve a lot of makeup problems, too, because you'll stick with one tone-group.

Lest you think this color-smart way of dressing is boring, I assure you it's not. Those of us who do it find it exciting to know we look our best. We're always on the lookout for bargains in our color group and no longer are tempted to impulse-buy the inappropriate.

To illustrate: I fit into the golden grouping. Last week I found a bargain on a suit. It fit into my color group and looked great on me. And I knew that when I took it home, I already had three shirts, a pair of boots, shoes, purses, scarves, and jewelry to go with it.

Here's one last suggestion on saving time with clothing purchases. Get in the habit of buying through mail-order catalogs. Nowadays, they carry high-fashion clothing of good quality, and you can't beat the convenience of trying on clothes in the privacy of your own home. You eliminate the hassle of crowds and standing in line to get waited on. You can return what you don't want. Because there is usually a lapse of several days between order and delivery you must plan ahead—and anything that encourages planning has to be good.

STAYING IN SHAPE

You owe it to yourself to keep fit. Not only will exercise streamline your body and strengthen your muscles, but it will also improve your skin, your hair, and probably your disposition. A lazy, out-of-condition body cuts down on efficiency, and therefore we can't move as quickly through our scheduled tasks.

Put regular exercise periods into your schedule and don't slight them. If you can't afford twenty minutes, squeeze in five minutes, four times a day. By writing it into your daily schedule as a fixed activity, you're more likely to do it so you can cross it off.

Establish a system so that you can go through the exercises without having to concentrate on them. If you need exercise equipment, keep it where you'll use it. My personal exercise consists of thirty minutes of stretching and leg lifts, five days a week. I keep my exercise rug rolled up in my bedroom closet and the leg weights under the bed. When I don't have to go out early, I exercise right before showering and dressing in the morning. Otherwise, I exercise at bedtime. Thirty minutes a day may sound like a lot of time to spend on myself, but not when you think about how efficiently I expect this body to perform the rest of the day.

REST

The one area where we women think we can snatch a little time is by slighting sleep time. Those of us who take care of families often have little time alone, and we're tempted when everyone else has bedded down to try to fit one more activity into the schedule. Yet this is one use of our time that we absolutely must not compromise.

When we build up a sleep deficit it shows—first in the eyes, then the skin, then the disposition, and eventually in our ability to think clearly and perform efficiently. We do no one any favor by this sort of short-sighted self-sacrifice.

I know that God sometimes calls us to give that extra effort to a person in need. When He does, He gives us His supernatural strength to carry on. I also know that my body is God's dwelling place, and I do not honor Him by abusing it. Too many Christian women crusade against drug and alcohol abuse yet damage their bodies through overuse. And they do it in the name of serving Christ.

Determine what your sleep needs are. Six hours? Eight? Ten? Build that number of hours into your daily schedule. If you can't get it all in one stretch, then get it in naps. But get it.

It's hard to store up sleep in advance. You're just not sleepy, right? As you schedule your days, plan to make up lost sleep on the day following the day you've deprived yourself. Explain to your family that your state of health requires this make-up time. Then don't let anything short of a house fire interfere. Nobody said your nap has to be mid-afternoon. Consider mid-morning, over the lunch hour (often more beneficial than food), or right after dinner. Keep a neck pillow in the car and nap while someone else drives (impossible if the driver also happens to be a teenager with a new license). Nap while you wait for that child at music lessons. I have been accused of napping while waiting for a traffic light to change.

Accept the fact that some people won't understand. They may ridicule you or try to make you feel guilty.

Your family, once they see that you mean business and have a better disposition when you get enough rest, will start to protect your rest time.

If you think it's impossible to do all that needs doing and still get enough sleep, then you're doing too much. Go back to Chapter 2 and work over your priorities again.

Control your time by deciding who's in charge. Save time by constantly seeking a more efficient way. Then take time to take care of yourself.

12 Time for M.E. (Meditation and Evaluation)

A wonderful thing happened to our son this summer when he went off for six weeks on the Georgia Governor's Honors Program. In addition to intensive study in his specialized field and a broad spectrum of enrichment studies, the daily schedule included an hour and a half after lunch of "Time for M.E." The wise planners of the program insisted that students spend this time outside the dormitories and classrooms, alone, without radio or musical instruments, in quiet. They were to use this time to think about life and their place in it.

For perhaps the first time in his busy teenage life, Steve had time to think. He thought about a lot of things. Over a period of several weeks we could see changes in his attitudes and opinions. If he got nothing else from the program, he found that "I can be alone and quiet. I need to be alone and quiet to get things sorted out."

God's woman needs this sort of time, too. The busier she is, the more she needs it. The Puritan work ethic has been so strongly ingrained in us that we suffer guilt pangs if we're not constantly kicking up the dust with our activities. We hear and take part in criticism of the woman who spends her off hours quietly, doing absolutely nothing.

We take the time to adorn our outsides and keep our surroundings clean, but we must guard against becoming beautiful empty shells. Without roots to anchor us, we wither up in the dry times or blow away in the storms.

I remember a dinner party several years ago. The food was delicious, the hostess gracious, the guests well-dressed. Do you know what we talked about? Our pets. After an hour of this I had to stifle a yawn. The second hour found my heart crying out, "People, is this all that's important to you? There are ideas to be explored. There are people hurting. The world is going to hell in a handbasket, and here we sit, talking about our dogs."

I'm not against pets. Ours have done some very amusing things. And I'm not an intellectual snob who thinks every conversation has to center on books and art. But my impression of the women (and many of the men) around that table was that they *had* nothing else to talk about. I was reminded of the story of the bear from the Northwest who decided to emigrate to a large southwestern state noted for its high opinion of itself. Obviously such a rich state would have plenty of tasty people for him to eat. In a few months, however, the bear was back home, looking emaciated. When asked what had happened, he replied, "Man, those folks are nothing but hats and boots." We need to take time to develop some substance in our lives so that we don't wind up as "hats and boots," with nothing but hot air in between.

We women, especially the nurturers, give out so much of ourselves that unless we recharge our batteries and refill our reservoirs, we do grow resentful—

sometimes without ever realizing it. We must take time for ourselves. I don't mean time for physical rest, or time to make ourselves look better. Nor do I mean time with God (I deal with this in another chapter). I mean time to discover who we are (and that's another book), time to create and recreate.

GETTING IN TOUCH WITH YOURSELF

What makes you tick? A complex inner clock which only God Himself could have designed. This clock doesn't just tell you when it's time to eat or sleep; it controls in repeating cycles your physical and emotional states. And because we often allow our physical and emotional states to influence our sense of spiritual well-being, it, too, seems to cycle through mountain tops and valleys.

I don't believe that an astrologer can predict your cycles by the zodiac sign under which you were born. Nor do I put much faith in the book which came with our new calculator when it tells me that given the date of my birth, I can figure out my cycles—twenty-three days for emotional, twenty-eight days for physical, and thirty-two days for intellectual cycles. I'm independent enough to want to think that God made my cycles, like my fingerprints, just a little different from everybody else born that day. I do believe that we can learn more about our individual ups and downs and plan to work with them.

By graphing my own physical and emotional state every day for several months, I was able to see a definite pattern. I could predict within a few days when my physical condition peaked so that I could take on a mountain of chores, and when it ebbed so that I was

Physical and Emotional Cycles Chart

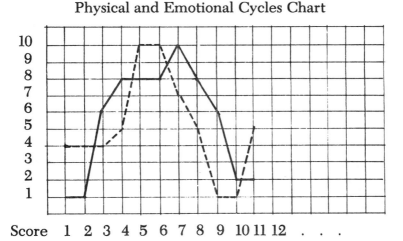

Score 1 2 3 4 5 6 7 8 9 10 11 12 . . .

Date: January

———————— = physical level, -------- = emotional level

Figure 3.

better off on the couch reading an English novel. I also learned the frequency of my emotional highs and lows. I knew that if I burst into tears because my husband asked where his socks were, it didn't mean our marriage was on the rocks. I accepted that my low day had arrived, and if he hadn't triggered it someone else would have.

Once armed with information about my ups and downs, I could schedule my time more intelligently. I stopped accepting speaking engagements for days when I knew I'd be a bundle of raw nerve ends. I saved window-washing for "tiger" days. Like budgeting my money and my time, I've learned to budget my energy and not spend it all in one place. I realize that with a family or a full-time job, it's not always possible, on those days, to crawl into your cave and put out the "Beware Mom" sign. I can't either. Then I pray a lot.

Make plans to take a reading of your own inner clock. Get some graph paper and date it as shown (p. 89). Use a sheet for physical cycles and another for emotional cycles, or plot them both on one by using different-colored lines. At the end of each day take stock and chart your physical and emotional levels on a scale of 1 to 10, with 10 being great and 1 being the pits. Do this for several months until you can see the pattern. Then use the results in scheduling your activities.

God gives each of us certain strengths (gifts) which He intends for us to use in His plan for us. Unfortunately, we've been told that modesty dictates our denying strengths, even when we know we have them. Some of us have even grown up thinking we have no strengths. Yet God has given them to us for His use and our pleasure. Once we can identify and affirm our strengths, we can harness them for using our time better.

Many of us are too ready to play up our weaknesses. Someone has told us that humility requires parading our faults before others and beating our breasts about them. Too often, we accept our weaknesses, using them as an excuse for doing and being less than God intended. As imperfect creatures born into an imperfect world, we are continually being shaped by God until one day, when we stand before Him, we'll be just like Jesus. He knows and works on our weaknesses. We must know them, too, in order to be aware of the ways they trap us.

Make a list of your own strengths and weaknesses. Do you have high physical energy levels? Are you good at analysis? Do you work better with people or alone? Do you procrastinate? What have other people told you you're good (or bad) at? Write it all down. Sometimes others can see us more clearly than we can see ourselves.

When you've completed your list, offer it to God. Thank Him for each of your strengths. Offer them to Him for His use, and ask Him to show you how to channel them. Then thank Him for your weaknesses. Acknowledge that He can use your weaknesses to perfect you. Ask Him to do it.

REBELLION—PLANNED AND UNPLANNED

About the time you think that you have it all under control—priorities, plans, schedules, systems, helpers—you'll experience a day when you'll say, "What a bore! Why do I have to live my whole life by a schedule? I want to be free!" And you'll feel like scrapping the whole thing. Expect this to happen. It will. I don't know what causes it. Maybe it's self-will rearing its ugly head or a strong ego asserting itself. Whatever the cause, it doesn't mean disaster if you, forewarned, know how to deal with it.

Go ahead and rebel—for a day, or even a week if you can afford it. When you've had your respite and worked through your rebellion at constant discipline, pick up your pen and your schedules and go on from there.

I think having no relief from a tightly disciplined life would send most of us 'round the bend. That's why we get these rebellious feelings. We can head off a lot of unscheduled rebellion by planning periods of respite into our schedules.

Anticipate the need for rest and make the time. Often, just knowing that you have a time of respite coming up soon will keep you going when you'd otherwise rebel. Right now, I'm looking ahead ten weeks to a period when I'll have put this book safely in the hands of the editor, and my employment will stop for several months. For two glorious weeks I plan to do nothing but entertain, be entertained, read, garden, tramp some hills, and renew friendships. In the meantime, I've reserved Sunday afternoons for M.E.

Use this M.E. time differently from the way you usually spend your time. If you live on a tight schedule, let this time be loose and unstructured. For example, when we go on vacation my husband likes to play golf. He likes me to play with him, and I enjoy the chance for us to spend five uninterrupted hours together. However, I refuse to play if he has reserved a tee time so early that I have to be on a schedule for getting up and eating breakfast in order to be on the golf course at a certain time. I spend my whole year meeting deadlines, and it's no vacation if I have to spend it meeting somebody else's schedule.

Don't feel guilty about taking this time for yourself. You'll be a better person for having done it. Just keep things in balance so that you get the time without growing overly self-indulgent.

Now, about those unscheduled rebellions. . . . Fortunately, they don't come too often. When someone counts on me to do a job, I'll usually get it done. It's the days when I don't have to answer to anyone about anything that I'm tempted to sloth.

Sometimes I can talk myself out of it (the schedule helps immensely). But when I can't, I settle back with a good book or putter around with a pair of pruning shears in my hand and let my body catch up with my spirit or the other way around. Some days, I bribe my-self into accomplishing a little. I read one chapter of a book. Then I lay the book aside and do one needleful of cross stitch. After that I get up and do the next thing on my list. Crossing the item off the list, I go on back for another chapter of reading.

As long as those days don't come too often, I refuse to feel guilty about them. I live a disciplined life the rest of the time. A lapse now and then into lethargy won't cause my world to fall in on itself. Those days probably make the schedule bearable the rest of the time, because even in the midst of my rebellion I'm aware that this is something I'm choosing to do. I'm still in control.

Time for me and time for M.E.—make them part of your total time control package.

13 Redeeming the Time

Recently, at a retreat with the theme of "Walk Closer," I taught a short seminar. My subject was finding time for God. The promotional literature and the retreat program clearly stated that we would explore ways of finding time to walk closer to God. Yet the participants who chose my seminar did so for several different reasons. Some had come to learn how to handle their time more wisely. Others had come because they had a vague feeling that they ought to walk closer to God, but never have the time. And then there were those who said, "I long to walk closer. Help me."

If you are reading this book for the first reason cited—to learn to handle your time more wisely—I hope you've found help. But don't stop there. You owe it to yourself to ask the question, "More time for what?"

Or, if you fit into the second group—the "I know I ought to spend more time with God but don't have time" folks—to you I say that we make time for what is important to us. Is time with God all that important? Let me answer that by asking a question. Does God welcome the stewardship of our time when it doesn't include time with Him? The place for you to start is not with finding time, but with finding the desire. The extent of a man's thirst is measured by how far he will go to get a drink. Just as you must learn the alphabet before you can read Shakespeare, just as you must crawl before you can walk, so you must develop a hunger and thirst for God before you'll be willing to make changes in your life patterns to allow time for Him.

Begin to pray that God's Spirit will create this sort of longing in you. Pray this prayer every day until you know that God has answered it with an insatiable desire for Himself, until you can say along with the psalmist, "My soul is athirst for God." Then go back to Chapter 1 with the full knowledge that because God desires your company even more than you desire His, He is willing to put His hand upon your setting of priorities.

To those of you who have already reached the third level of your spiritual maturity—the longing for more time with God—welcome. For you, I have some suggestions.

A SCHEDULE FOR GOD TIME? YOU BET!

The most successful way to find time for God is to make it. That is, write God into your schedule. By now, you should be planning each day on paper. Look over the plans. Ask God to show you the best time to meet Him. Then make a date with God for that time. To further commit yourself, tell someone—someone who cares about your spiritual growth and will ask you occasionally how you're doing. I find this act of commitment important. It's like going on a reducing diet. If you don't tell anyone you're dieting and then you cheat, no one knows. But if someone knows and is watching, you're more apt to stick to the diet.

I can't tell you the best time for your date with God. That depends on your lifestyle and metabolism. I (and many others) have found first thing in the morning best.

If I wait until the family arises, I have too many interruptions. If I save my devotional time for the end of the day, I find I'm doing an awful lot of praying after-the-fact. With the schedule I keep, with teenagers going out into a world of temptation, with a husband who must deal with the stresses of the business world, I want to make sure I pray for all of us before we put the day into gear.

Once you've committed yourself to a daily quiet time, you can count on Satan's trying to destroy it. He won't use repulsive means. Instead he'll present you with all sorts of worthwhile activities—things which need doing—to lure you away. Funny, isn't it, how Satan doesn't really bother with you until you get serious about knowing God better. I've noticed at least two ways Satan has of torpedoing my efforts.

One way is to keep me up late at night so that I find it almost physically impossible to get up early. Just a few days ago, one of our children needed to talk. My husband was out of town, and I was in bed, writing in my journal. The child stood in the doorway, asking questions, and then finally gravitated toward the bedroom chair. We talked and talked and talked. It was a precious time of sharing. I think I communicated some values and received something in return. When we finally looked at the clock, it registered 1:00 A.M. We were both shocked.

Getting up at 5:30 the next morning was work, but I

managed. The day's schedule had no time for a nap. That night, my husband returned home needing his share of attention—physical and emotional—and another late night ensued. The following morning, when the alarm sounded, all I could do was moan, "Forgive me, Lord," and reset the alarm. I managed to slip in twenty minutes for God after everybody had cleared the house, but even that was interrupted by the telephone. Yet the reasons for my getting to bed late were certainly worthwhile.

Satan has a way of also getting to me on the other end. I rise early in order to be alone, but it doesn't always work out that way. Because our house doesn't have too many places where I can be alone, I have my quiet time in the kitchen in cold weather and on the glassed-in porch when it's warm. I find myself some mornings trying to pray while one child, who has gotten up early to finish some homework, studies at the dining room table and the other child, who has forgotten to tell me about an early band rehearsal, starts the shower and announces that he needs breakfast in fifteen minutes and asks to use my car since his is out of gas. At times I have locked myself in the downstairs powder room just long enough to say, "Help!"

I don't know enough theology to split hairs over how much of this Satan causes and how much we bring on ourselves. But I do know that Satan will scuttle my budget if he can. I'm engaged in holy warfare. My reinforcements come from the quiet time. One of the battlegrounds is my schedule.

As well as putting time for God into your budget, you can take advantage of the ready-made times. Your Sunday and midweek church services provide a chance to worship and praise. These few hours we spend assembled as the Body of Christ are not enough, but they do contribute toward the total time we give to God.

Then, just as we have learned to utilize the fragments of time for other purposes, we must learn to use them as opportunities to touch base with God.

Though it can never take the place of those glorious uninterrupted times of deep communion with God, we mustn't sell short the idea of praying in fragments. If we were to keep track of all the minutes and half minutes we spend in prayer each day, we would find they do add up. Our mistake is in thinking that unless we have long, uninterrupted blocks of time, we haven't been with God.

Brother Lawrence, a fifteenth-century French monk, had almost perfected this means of staying in touch with God. In his book, *The Practice of the Presence of God,* he wrote, "The time of business does not with me differ from the time of prayer; and in the noise of my kitchen, while several persons are at the same time calling for different things, I possess God in as great tranquility as if I were upon my knees at the blessed sacrament."

I shall never, in this life, approach Brother Lawrence's closeness to God, but I continue to work at practicing the Presence. Two things help. First, the habit of continually thanking God for the small and seemingly insignificant details. And second, asking His opinion of things. I've printed a little card which stands on my desk. It says, "Referral and Consultation." I'm sure, to my co-workers, that it looks like a reminder for a doctor's appointment. Actually, it reminds me as I complete a task to refer to God, to thank Him for His help in it, and to consult Him on what job to do next and how.

AND A SYSTEM, TOO

It is not enough that we set aside time to be with God. We must use that time wisely or we'll find that Satan has stolen it from us. We'll have daydreamed it away or spent it on the nonessentials. As well as a time, we must have a place and a plan.

Choose a pleasant place, free of distractions, for your quiet time. Form the habit of always going to the same place. Soon, because of its familiarity, you'll be able to tune out your surroundings and concentrate upon God. Cultivate the place long enough and you'll find you can slip into a devotional frame of mind as easily as you slip into a chair. Keep your materials—Bibles, commentaries, prayer lists, notebook, and pencils—nearby so that you don't spend precious minutes of your allotted time rounding them up.

You'll need to think about two aspects of your quiet time—its duration and how you allot it. If you've not been in the habit of keeping a daily devotional time, don't start out overambitiously. If you resolve to spend thirty minutes, it may require such a drastic adjustment to your schedule that you'll abandon the whole idea. Or, you might find that you've finished in five minutes and have twenty-five minutes to feel guilty for not having more to say to God.

Better to start out with six minutes and increase it gradually as your need for more time with God increases. If you have to get up earlier than was your custom, six minutes doesn't seem like nearly the sacrifice that thirty does.

Your devotional plan means that you know what you want to do and go immediately to it without wasting time. It also means that you balance your time and don't get so caught up in reading that you have no time to pray, or vice versa. I divide my time into three equal segments. That's why I recommended scheduling an even number of minutes.

In the first segment, I study the Bible (further subdivided into one Old Testament chapter, one New Testament chapter portion, and one psalm. I break down the long psalms and New Testament chapters, which are packed with more ideas than I can handle at one sitting, into smaller reading assignments.). Because I take notes on my reading, I know right where I've left off. My notes also refresh my memory about the preceding studies.

The second portion of my quiet time I devote to reading what other Christians have written. I believe that God still inspires men and women to write about Him, and although their writings don't add to or subtract from the Scriptures, they inspire me and contribute to my understanding. I like to vary my reading from classic to contemporary; from Augustine, to Hannah Whithall Smith, to Catherine Marshall, and a host of others. I have to discipline myself during this portion, because I can get carried away with my reading and slight my prayer time.

That brings me to the shortest twenty minutes of my day—my time of conversing with God. Even here, I find a plan saves me time and keeps my mind from wandering. I don't know who first came up with the idea of using the acronym ACTS (adoration, confession, thanksgiving, and supplication) as a prayer guide. Whoever you are, thank you. ACTS keeps me praying purposefully and in the right order. The four letters of ACTS also remind me that only one-fourth of my prayers should ask for things. The other three-fourths should concentrate on God and my place in His plan.

I have certain items I pray about every day—my own spiritual condition, my family, our church leaders, my schedule and my work, the members of our small group. I pray about other things on alternate days. On Monday, Wednesday, and Friday, I pray about my goals for the year and the month. These days find me praying specifically about the band boosters, my writing, and whatever else I've listed as goals.

On Tuesday, Thursday, and Saturday, I pray for those on my intercessory list. I also pray for the special groups I'm committed to—Sunday school class, discipleship class, or missions groups. I have never taken lightly my promise to pray for someone. I write it down and I do it. Consequently, my intercessory list gets pretty long at times, but I'd hate to think that someone was depending on my prayers and I had forgotten them.

I save the last few minutes of each prayer time for God to talk to me. I just stay quiet and listen. In my mind, I hear Him speak—often with a verse of Scripture, a promise, a direction. I write it down and date it for future reference.

If you are thinking that my devotional time sounds awfully regimented or lacking in spontaneity, I assure you that it's not. By managing all the details I free my mind from the worry that I've forgotten something. Besides, I can't find anything in the Bible that tells us to pray only when we feel like it or to pray only about that which pops into our minds. If I were to do that, prayer would soon cease to be a part of my life—it would be crowded right out.

I think God is important enough to make time for Him, to put Him into my schedule. I like to think He likes it that way, too.

TIME FOR CLIMBING MOUNTAINS

In several passages throughout the gospels, we read of Jesus' separating Himself from the crowds. "And when he had sent the multitudes away, he went up into a mountain apart to pray: and when the evening was come, he was there alone" (Matt. 14:23, KJV). "But he slipped quietly away to deserted places for prayer" (Luke 15:16, Phillips).

I find that I, too, need my times in the mountains. Group worship, practicing the Presence, and keeping the daily quiet time all help. But the larger chunk of time spent with God helps me take a long look at the total picture of my life and keeps me from bogging down in the details of daily living.

I schedule a half-day retreat for myself at the beginning of each month. I write it on my calendar, and when the time comes I gather Bible, hymnal, note books, and pen, and I leave home. That's a must. I don't want the distraction of a ringing telephone or doorbell or the sight of a cobweb to lure me away from my intended retreat.

In good weather, I take a blanket and sit in a nearby park. Bad weather may find me in the public library, the prayer room of the church, in the parked car—but away and quiet. I spend the time reading my Bible, praying, reading hymns, evaluating progress on last month's goals, and formulating ones for the coming month.

I usually find a specific Scripture which I can claim as a promise and run to for refuge throughout the next month. I also try to find a hymn which will speak to me. Singing and reading it for a whole month commits it to memory—one more aid programmed into my mental computer to be retrieved when needed.

I use this time, after setting goals, to plan the month in as much detail as I can—even down to what to wear, and when. Sometimes I have to change the plans as I go. But knowing I have them, and that God and I have made them together, gives me a great feeling of control over the next month.

Working women will find it hard to set aside that larger chunk, but do it. An evening, a Saturday morning, a Sunday afternoon, whenever—but schedule it. When I returned to the world of the gainfully employed recently, I let a month slip by without scheduling my retreat. It seemed that I couldn't indulge myself with half a day. That's when the events described in Chapter 10 transpired. Now I realize the necessity of the retreat and I'm back in control, but it was a tough fight.

You see, it was when I began to spend time with God that He enabled me to get a grip on myself, to see clearly where He wanted me to go and what He wanted me to do. As I gave Him my few moments, He taught me how to handle the hours and the days. When I handled them better, I had more time for Him and His will. And the more time I committed to Him, the more He expanded the time to fill my need for it. It has turned into one grand and glorious cycle of my giving my days to God and His stretching them and giving them back with just enough room in each of them for me to grow a little.

I've found that the more the day needs stretching, the more time I must spend with God. The temptation, of course, is to get more time by cutting out God's share. Oh, I haven't reached the peak of Martin Luther, who once said, "I have so much to do (today) that I shall spend the first three hours in prayer." After all, Luther sparked the Reformation. I despair of reforming even two sloppy kids. But I believe that God intends for my life (and yours), as it keeps on growing, to be just as abundant and productive as was Luther's. That abundance will only come as we get to know, intimately, the Giver of Abundant Life, the Creator and Redeemer of Time. And that takes time.

14 The Fullness of Time

As we get more and better control of our time, we have more to say in how we use it. Then we have to make choices about whether we'll spend it preparing for the future or enjoying the present.

We find people on both sides of the argument. The bankers tell us to save for a rainy day. Credit card companies urge us to go now and pay later. One slogan warns us that the future belongs to those who prepare for it, while another old bromide says, "Gather ye rosebuds while ye may."

One day several years ago found me feverishly making strawberry jam for the freezer, then serving canned peaches for dessert at dinner. When my husband asked, "Where have all the strawberries gone?" I had to confess, "I made jam with them." I was so busy storing up for the future that I had used up all of today's pleasure for tomorrow's security.

But I also remember Aesop's fable of the ant and the grasshopper. All summer long, the grasshopper sat on a blade of grass and strummed his guitar while the ant industriously stored food for the approaching winter. When the ant scolded the grasshopper for not preparing for the future, the grasshopper answered that he felt his music was more important. Later, when the snow covered the ground, the grasshopper asked the ant for something to eat, and the ant told him to "bug off."

Which side is right? They both are. We must strike a balance between grasshopper and ant—savoring the taste of fresh strawberries and yet putting some jam away for later. I don't have a schedule or a system to help you. Playing grasshopper one day and ant the next is a tough act. It's much easier to be one or the other all the time.

God tells us, "To everything there is a season, and a time to every purpose." His Spirit, when we allow Him to fill and control our lives, will give us the sensitivity to know when to eat and when to preserve.

I had a good example of this as I moonlighted on this book, held a full-time job, celebrated Christmas, kept the family in food and clothes, and nursed our daughter who had been felled by mononucleosis. The enforced quietness of her recuperation had given our patient housefever. Several times she came to the door of the room where I write and asked, "Want to play a game?"

After my turning her down two or three times, that still small voice inside said, "Hey, wait a minute. Who has the higher priority, your daughter or your publisher?"

I realized that the season had come to spend some time with our children. I put down my pen and we played a game. Then our son wanted me to play table tennis with him. He beat me, of course. I couldn't really afford to spend the time, but I couldn't afford not to, either. When our son is away at college, he won't need me for a table tennis partner, and our daughter, when well, has friends with whom she'd prefer to play games.

In addition to there being a right season for everything, I've noticed something else about the seasons. They change. And they keep on changing. God's woman must change with them, embracing the experiences of each new season instead of clinging to the past. Cute as our babies were, as much fun as their childhood brought us, their failure to mature into adolescence and adulthood would be utter tragedy.

Accept the passing of time and the changes it brings. Take care of yourself physically, emotionally, and spiritually, but realize that you can't remain forever in blue jeans. There's something sad about a grandmother who tries to pass herself off as a teenager. Frankly, I don't mind if people know that my hair color comes out of a bottle, and that underneath it all I'm gray. I've earned every one of those gray hairs. Right now, I think I look better with brown hair, but when the aging of my skin catches up with the aging of my hair color, I hope I'll have the good sense to embrace that season, too.

We can't step into a time-warp and go back to relive our past. We need, therefore, to live in such a way that we can look at the past without regret. I'd like to suggest some ways to do that.

STOP AND SMELL THE ROSES ALONG THE WAY

Develop a heightened sense of awareness in all you do. Be sensitive to sights, sounds, colors, and smells. Savor each moment in the midst of your busyness. The noise and mess of teenagers, the furry-dog smell of a sweaty little boy—store up the memories. You may never pass that way again.

Yesterday, I planted my tomato plants. I felt the sun warming my body. The perspiration trickled down between my shoulder blades, and my scalp prickled with moisture. I smelled the honeysuckle blooming on the neighbor's fence and listened to the chirping of robins, the singing of bluebirds, the shrieking of jays, and the squawking of mocking birds as they divebombed the cat, and she in turn swished her tail in absolute disdain. I ate a sun-warmed strawberry or two. Then, pulling a radish and washing it at the garden hose, I tasted its pungency.

A Japanese gentleman once said, "One difference between Americans and Japanese in the garden is that you say you work in the garden. We say we garden. We don't call it work."

Yesterday, I gardened. Next winter, as I look out on the bleakness and huddle up to the fireplace, I'll remember yesterday. I may open a jar of homegrown tomatoes to add to the soup, but I'll remember the sun and the birds, and I'll be filled with more than food.

STAY LOOSE

Make sure your commitments and your schedules aren't so rigid that you can't adjust them. I'm not saying don't commit yourself. A sense of commitment makes the difference between success and failure on the job, in your marriage, and certainly in your Christian growth. But examine your commitments periodically to see if they need refocusing.

My husband came to his senses on this issue long before I did. One choir director just couldn't understand when my husband dropped out of choir for a few years in order to coach our son's soccer team.

"But choir is the Lord's work," the director protested.

"So is my relationship with my son," my husband answered.

Father and son have progressed to other things now. No longer does the dad help his lad with Boy Scout merit badges. Nor does he teach soccer skills and strategy—a high school coach has taken his place, and Dad can only sit in the stands and cheer or moan. Instead, they work together to keep the boy's vintage automobile running. Some precious conversations between grease-smeared father and son have taken place over a torn-down carburetor.

My husband sings in the choir again now, but he told me today that he'll go to the high school soccer game tomorrow night. When I reminded him that it was choir night, he quietly said, "I know. And Steve has only two games left to play before graduation. I want to be there."

QUALITY COMPENSATES FOR QUANTITY

Give quality time to your family. Try, when you're with your family, to be really with them.

I recall being seated at the dinner table one night when I became aware of a voice, as if from a great distance, saying, "Earth to Mrs. Miller ... Earth to Mrs. Miller. . . ." Then someone snapped his fingers in front of my staring, unblinking eyes. As I tore myself away from whatever list or paragraph I was composing and returned to planet earth, I heard laughter. That time, my family thought my mental checkout was funny. They don't always.

Get the mundane out of the way while your family

isn't around so that you can give them your undivided attention when they are. I try to give the appearance of doing nothing when the children arrive home from school. When I hear the screech of the school bus brakes, I drop what I'm doing and sit down with a piece of needlework or a book or a basket of laundry to fold. A child, seeing my attention not deeply engaged in something, is encouraged to sit down for a chat. In a few minutes, when the child goes on to his own activities, I resume whatever it was I had dropped.

I also try to schedule the dinner preparations so that I can leave the kitchen for a few minutes and sit in the living room with my husband when he gets home. If dinner is going to be delayed because of someone's schedule, I fix us a glass of tomato juice. After a few minutes of chat, he reads the newspapers and I return to the kitchen.

This doesn't always work. I get my priorities out of order, too. Last night found us meeting at the local chain restaurant for a quick hamburger between meetings. When we finally got home (in separate cars), I went to the kitchen. My husband followed me there, but I was busy with breakfast preparations. Then, when we climbed into bed, I had my nose in a book that was overdue at the library. Finally, my husband blurted out, "Well, my boss announced today that I'm being considered for a promotion." Well, he got my attention. Up until then, I'd spent my time making sure of food and clothing and schedules, but I hadn't given my husband any quality time.

Give quality time to the Family of God. Unlike cleanliness, busyness—inside or outside the church—is not next to godliness. We use too much of our time in the church just turning the wheels, greasing the machinery so that the organization keeps humming along, perpetuating itself.

Jesus reproved Martha for this sort of busyness. Mary, He said, had chosen to spend her time on quality (Luke 10:38-42). Make sure that you give "Mary" time and not "Martha" time to your church. If it's quality, you needn't feel guilty about the quantity of it. Find out what God has for you to do, then do it with all your might.

When I first began to direct our church's ministry to internationals, I had to say no to a lot of other worthwhile jobs. Some people couldn't understand why I no longer taught a Sunday school class or attended every meeting. Yet I believed that God had called me out to do this job, that He had brought my gifts, my education, and my personality all into focus on this one need. It's nice to be wanted, it's worth a lot of ego strokes, but I had to learn that I could either be a missionary or go to missionary meetings.

Then give quality time to those outside the Family of God so that you present them with a clear, unmistakable picture of Jesus. I don't mean preach a sermon or buttonhole someone and say, "Sister, are you saved?" I do mean a glow, an interest, a caring for other persons. I mean a courtesy, a warm willingness to let someone else go first. I mean a radiant difference in your attitude which provokes them to say, as did one of my international students, "There's something different about you. You have a peace and joy that I don't have."

To which I replied, "Yes, the difference is God's presence in my life." Today, I count that Belgian woman as a sister in the Family of God because God allowed me to spend some quality time with her.

TAKE TIME TO DECIDE

In the fullness of time, God sent forth His Son. Scholars have speculated that the time—historically, politically, and theologically—was right for the gospel to spread throughout the world.

I believe that in the fullness of this, another time, you picked up this book and began to read it. Not by chance, but by divine design. For as I've written, I've pictured you in my mind, and I've prayed that God would use these words to help you get control of your time.

To everything there is a season, and to every purpose a time. Could this be the time for you to take control? Could this be the season for you to say, "It's about time"?

CHRISTIAN HERALD ASSOCIATION AND ITS MINISTRIES

CHRISTIAN HERALD ASSOCIATION, founded in 1878, publishes The Christian Herald Magazine, one of the leading interdenominational religious monthlies in America. Through its wide circulation, it brings inspiring articles and the latest news of religious developments to many families. From the magazine's pages came the initiative for CHRISTIAN HERALD CHILDREN'S HOME and THE BOWERY MISSION, two individually supported not-for-profit corporations.

CHRISTIAN HERALD CHILDREN'S HOME, established in 1894, is the name for a unique and dynamic ministry to disadvantaged children, offering hope and opportunities which would not otherwise be available for reasons of poverty and neglect. The goal is to develop each child's potential and to demonstrate Christian compassion and understanding to children in need.

Mont Lawn is a permanent camp located in Bushkill, Pennsylvania. It is the focal point of a ministry which provides a healthful "vacation with a purpose" to children who without it would be confined to the streets of the city. Up to 1000 children between the ages of 7 and 11 come to Mont Lawn each year.

Christian Herald Children's Home maintains year-round contact with children by means of an *In-City Youth Ministry*. Central to its philosophy is the belief that only through sustained relationships and demonstrated concern can individual lives be truly enriched. Special emphasis is on individual guidance, spiritual and family counseling and tutoring. This follow-up ministry to inner-city children culminates for many in financial assistance toward higher education and career counseling.

THE BOWERY MISSION, located at 227 Bowery, New York City, has since 1879 been reaching out to the lost men on the Bowery, offering them what could be their last chance to rebuild their lives. Every man is fed, clothed and ministered to. Countless numbers have entered the 90-day residential rehabilitation program at the Bowery Mission. A concentrated ministry of counseling, medical care, nutrition therapy, Bible study and Gospel services awakens a man to spiritual renewal within himself.

These ministries are supported solely by the voluntary contributions of individuals and by legacies and bequests. Contributions are tax deductible. Checks should be made out either to CHRISTIAN HERALD CHILDREN'S HOME or to THE BOWERY MISSION.

Administrative Office: 40 Overlook Drive, Chappaqua, New York 10514
Telephone: (914) 769-9000